CAMBRIDGE SKILLS FOR FLUENCY
Series Editor: Adrian Doff

Listening 4

Adrian Doff
Christopher Jones

CAMBRIDGE
UNIVERSITY PRESS

PUBLISHED BY THE PRESS SYNDICATE OF THE UNIVERSITY OF CAMBRIDGE
The Pitt Building, Trumpington Street, Cambridge CB2 1RP, United Kingdom

CAMBRIDGE UNIVERSITY PRESS
The Edinburgh Building, Cambridge CB2 1RU, United Kingdom
40 West 20th Street, New York, NY 10011–4211, USA
10 Stamford Road, Oakleigh, Melbourne 3166, Australia

First published 1995
Reprinted 1997

Printed in Great Britain at the University Press, Cambridge

ISBN 0 521 36750 6 Book
ISBN 0 521 36547 3 Cassettes

Contents

Map of the book

Unit	Contents	Vocabulary/ topic areas	Listening strategies/activities
1 I was scared to death	Part of a *Dracula* story; description of a horror film; radio discussion	Films; horror	Following a story; predicting; matching with your own opinion
2 Family life (1)	People commenting on their upbringing; people remembering their childhood	The family; childhood; remembering the past	Matching with your own experience and opinion
3 The sound of selling	An interview about writing music for TV commercials; extracts from commercials	Advertising; music; television	Listening to an unfamiliar subject; identifying topic
4 The island	An actor reading an American Indian short story	Narrative	Following a story; predicting; listening for details
5 Far from home	English people describing the experience of living in Germany and Malaysia	Foreign countries; customs; food	Matching with your own experience; predicting and guessing
6 The Louvre Pyramid	An evaluation of the Louvre Pyramid; people presenting plans for alternatives	Architecture; amenities in towns	Matching with your own opinion; evaluating what you hear
7 Technically speaking	A series of short technical explanations; an explanation of how to do kite racing	Medicine; cookery; sport	Following a technical explanation; understanding a foreign accent
8 GWR FM	Excerpts from local radio; a developing news story	Radio; advertising; news; crime	Identifying topic; listening for general idea; listening for specific information
9 Loud and aggressive	Recent developments in popular music; part of a song by the Henry Rollins Band	Popular music; attitudes	Matching with your own knowledge/opinion; catching the words of a song

Unit		Contents	Vocabulary/ topic areas	Listening strategies/activities
10	Sarajevo	Three people describing their experience of living in Sarajevo in 1992-3	War; human qualities	Matching with your own knowledge; understanding implied meaning
11	Out West	An American tracing his family history; anecdotes about his great grandmother	History; family relationships; the USA	Following a narrative; listening for specific information
12	Jigsaw of a village	People talking about their jobs and lifestyle; recordings of everyday activities	Jobs; village life	Listening for main points; interpreting what's going on (with background noise)
13	All you need is love?	Someone commenting on relationships; a description of an arranged marriage	Love; relationships; marriage	Matching with your own opinion
14	Get it?	Children's jokes; a classic comedy performance	Humour	Understanding rapid speech; catching the point of a joke; following a story
15	In black and white (1)	A lecture about print-making techniques	Art; technical processes	Listening for main points; listening and note-taking
16	In black and white (2)	Interpretation of a picture; the artist talking about the picture	Art	Matching with your own opinion; predicting and guessing
17	*The Great Ruby Robbery (1)*	Part 1 of a radio drama based on a Victorian detective story	Crime; the law	Following an extended story; predicting and guessing
18	*The Great Ruby Robbery (2)*	Part 2 of the radio drama	Crime; the law	Following an extended story; predicting and guessing
19	Family life (2)	Mother and daughter discussing conflicts	Everyday activities; education	Listening for general idea; evaluating an argument
20	*Here*	A poem by Philip Larkin; someone talking about the poem	Towns; the countryside; homesickness; poetry	Interpreting poetic language; understanding implied meaning

1 | I was scared to death

Horror films and why people like them

A Dracula

1   Work in groups. What do you know about
    Count Dracula? Add to these notes:

    He wears black. He drinks blood …

2   You will hear some extracts from the original novel by Bram Stoker.
    The recording is in two parts.

    Here are some words that you will hear in the first part. Before you listen,
    match the words on the left with those on the right.

pointed	howling	rattling		teeth	ears	castle
sharp	cruel			breath	wolves	
rank (= foul-smelling)		ruined		chains	mouth	

    Now listen to the first part and check your answers.

    What other things add to the creepy atmosphere of the story?

6

8/may
12/may

• no Reflection
• demon-like fur)
  – throat
• not eat/drink
• crawl down wall
• cloak/wings

3 [cassette] Listen to the second part, and answer these questions:

What makes the visitor realise that Dracula is not a normal human being?
What expressions does he use that show that he is frightened?

4 Why do you think people find Dracula films frightening?
Do you find them frightening?

B *The Vanishing*

1 You will hear someone describing a film called *The Vanishing*.
Before you listen, look at the words below, which are all elements in the story.

ab

a holiday	the murderer
the girlfriend	a petrol station
the boyfriend	a coffin
a picnic	a lighter

[cassette] Now listen to the story. How do the elements fit together?

2 Here are some expressions the speaker used. What do they mean?

1 she was abducted by a sicko
2 his family was romping and frolicking
3 obsessive search for his girlfriend
4 a low-key matter-of-fact way
5 totally chilling
6 it gave me the creeps

3 Which scene does the speaker find most frightening?
Why does she find it so frightening?

4 Why do you think people find films like *The Vanishing* frightening?
Do you find them frightening?

C Extension: Why do people watch horror films?

1 Read some possible reasons why people watch horror films.

A It isn't the horror films themselves that people enjoy, but the feeling afterwards when they come back to reality and realise they are safe after all.

B Everyone has deep subconscious fears. Seeing horror films helps us to confront those fears and deal with them in a harmless way.

C People don't have enough danger and excitement in their everyday lives, so they need the substitute excitement that horror films provide.

D People see horror films because they find them entertaining – they're so far removed from reality that people don't take them seriously.

E We find it fascinating to watch something terrible happening to someone else – it makes us feel good that it isn't happening to us.

2 You will hear part of a radio discussion about why people enjoy horror films. Which of the reasons above are mentioned?

3 Which of the points the speakers make do you think would apply to Dracula films?
Which would apply to *The Vanishing*?

genre
• suspense
• voyeurism
• tabloids
• unravelling of the past

8

2 | Family life (1)

Some adults look back on their childhood

A The perfect parent

1   Here are four pairs of opposite opinions about bringing up children. Which
do you agree with more? For each pair of statements, mark an ✕ on the line
to show where your own opinion lies.

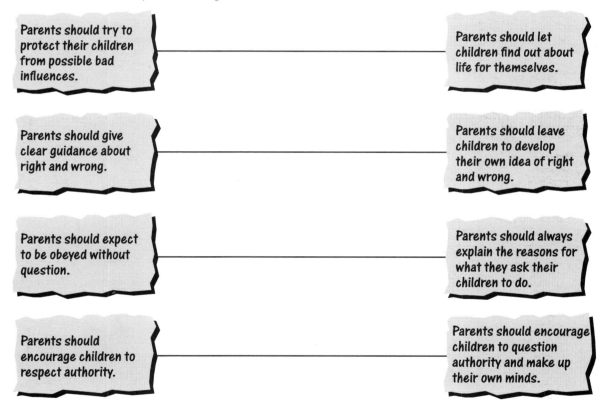

Parents should try to protect their children from possible bad influences.

Parents should let children find out about life for themselves.

Parents should give clear guidance about right and wrong.

Parents should leave children to develop their own idea of right and wrong.

Parents should expect to be obeyed without question.

Parents should always explain the reasons for what they ask their children to do.

Parents should encourage children to respect authority.

Parents should encourage children to question authority and make up their own minds.

Now join your ✕s together to give yourself an 'opinion profile'. Then find
someone with a different profile from you. Compare your opinions.

2   [cassette icon] You will hear two adults talking about how their parents brought
them up. Listen and decide where they would mark their opinions on the
scale above.

What did the speakers say that made you decide on your answers?

3   Look at the expressions below. What do they mean?
    How did the speakers use them?

    Speaker 1   *Speaker 2*
    a bit of a cop-out   hang out
    a strict disciplinary code   lenient
    a narrow way of thinking   Spare the rod and spoil the child
    a lack of common ground   a very rough crowd

    If necessary, listen again and check your answers.

B Brothers and sisters

1   What do you think are the main advantages and disadvantages of being:
    – an only child?
    – one of a large number of brothers and sisters?
    – the oldest child?
    – the youngest child?

2   ▭ You will hear four people talking about their position in their family as
    children, and how they felt about it. Listen and complete the table.

	Position in family	Plus points	Minus points
Roger	one of 9	Had a good time	
Tasia	Youngest of 5		
Hazel			
Chris			Sometimes lonely

10

3 Which of the four people do you think would be most likely to say these things?

a) Perhaps I got my own way a bit too much as a child.
b) I often felt envious of my brothers and sisters.
c) Everyone treated me as the baby of the family.
d) My parents were often short of money.
e) My father was quite strict.
f) I used to dream of being bought a new dress.
g) Everyone thought I was a clever child.

What did they say that made you choose your answers?

4 Which of the speakers seems to be:

– the most satisfied about his/her childhood?
– the least satisfied about his/her childhood?

C Extension: Your own childhood

1 Think about what the speakers in Section A said about their parents.
How would you describe your own parents' attitudes to bringing you up?
Do you think they were too strict? not strict enough? about right?

2 Think about your own position in your family when you were a child.
How would you complete the table in Section B?
Which of the four speakers do you think you have most in common with?

3 One of the speakers in Section B enjoys privacy because he didn't have it as a child; another speaker enjoys privacy because he came to expect it as a child.

In what ways do you think your childhood has influenced you as an adult?

3 | The sound of selling

Making the music for TV commercials

A Catchy tunes

🎵 You will hear three short tunes by Graham Preskett, a composer who writes music for TV commercials. Listen to each tune, and imagine it being used in a TV commercial.

What kind of product do you think it might be advertising?
Why do you think so?

B At the keyboard

1   🎵 You will hear an interview in which Graham talks about his work. The interview is in four parts. Listen to each part and answer the questions.

Part 1
What does Graham say music is used for in TV commercials?
What is a jingle?

Part 2

According to Graham, what kind of music would be suitable for each of these products? Make brief notes.

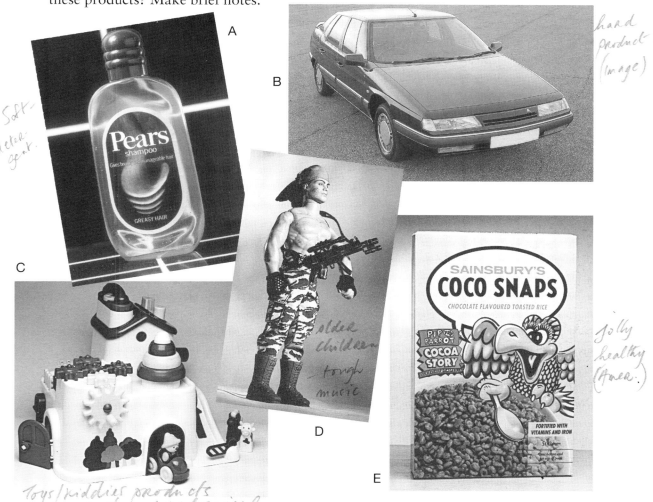

A

B — *hard product (image)*

Soft detergent. — A (Pears shampoo)

C — *Toys/kiddies products jingly mechanical*

D — *older children tough music*

E — *Jolly healthy (Amer.)* (Sainsbury's Coco Snaps)

Which three tunes were the ones you heard in Section A?

Part 3

Which words was Graham told to incorporate into the Tia Maria commercial?

What kind of 'image' is created by the commercial?

Sun, sand, sea 'soul'

Part 4

At what stages does Graham get paid for his music? Make a list.

2 Which of these words do you think best describe Graham's feelings about his work?

involved	cynical	enthusiastic
confident	bored	embarrassed

13

C The finished product

📼 You will hear a complete TV commercial for which Graham wrote the music.

What product is being advertised?
What do you imagine happening on the screen?
What kind of 'image' do the words and the music project?

D Extension activities

1 Are there any TV commercials you remember because of the music?
How is the music related to the product?

2 Which of these statements about TV advertising do you agree with (if any)?

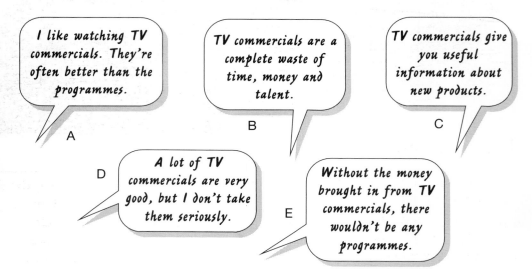

3 Think of a product and write the words for a jingle.
If you like, make up a tune to go with it.

14

4 | The island

A traditional Iroquois Indian tale

A The first half of the story

1   You will hear the first half of a story about an Iroquois Indian boy.

Before you listen, look at the picture and read the questions and the list of key words (which are all in the right order). How much can you guess about what you're going to hear?

verbs

1 Where did the boy live? *hut*
2 What was he allowed to do?
3 What wasn't he allowed to do?
4 What did he do one day? Why?
5 Why was the lake dangerous?
6 The man and the boy did three things together. What were they?
7 How did the man call the boat?
8 What happened when they reached the island?
9 How badly was the boy injured?
10 What was there to eat?
11 What did the voice ask him to do?

savage fish
fins swirl

ached from the fists

2   ▭ Now listen and answer the questions in Exercise 1.

Key words
boy
father
lake
drink
fish
man
spear
island
whistled
boat
swans
bruises
fists
berries
dig
voice

B The second half of the story

1   Here are some key words from the second half of the story.
    Try to imagine roughly what will happen.

Part 1	skeleton – tobacco – pipe – mouse
Part 2	man – dogs – tree
Part 3	night – man – blood – hole – sand – boat

2   [cassette] Listen to the second half of the story. At each break, say what you
    think will happen next.

3   Here are some phrases from the second half of the story.
    How many do you know the meaning of?

    1 the boy was startled   4 there's a pouch   7 leaving tracks
    2 in the leaf-mould   5 in my ribs   8 his scent was everywhere
    3 just by the bole   6 such a torment   9 the boat is beached

    If necessary, listen to the story again.

4   Make up an ending for the story.

    [cassette] Now listen to the last part of the story.
    How similar was it to your own ending?

C Extension: Interpreting the story

1   What do you think the story is about? Look at the opinions below. Which
    of them (if any) do you agree with? Think of events in the story which
    support your interpretation.

    a) It's about growing up and becoming a man.
    b) It's about learning to survive alone.
    c) It's about the forces of evil, and how to overcome them.
    d) It's about respecting your ancestors, and how they can help you.
    e) It's about what happens to you after you die.

2   The story was read by Vincent Price, who is best known
    as an actor in horror films.

    Do you think he was a good choice of reader?
    Did the way he read the story influence your interpretation of it?

5 | Far from home

The experience of living in a foreign country

A Living abroad

Imagine you have gone to live abroad in an English speaking country.
What things about the experience do you think would be exciting or would make you feel good?
What things would be difficult or might make you feel homesick?
Make two lists, then compare them with other people in the class.

B A foreigner in Germany

1   You will hear an English woman talking about the experience of living in Germany.

Which of these statements do you think she would agree with?

a) Living in Germany is much the same as living in Britain.
b) It's great to experience new things.
c) My German is excellent.
d) I find it easier to be assertive here than in Britain.
e) I don't feel integrated into German society.
f) I miss being in Britain.

2   According to the woman, what is difficult about:

– going to the doctor?
– going to the lost property office?
– listening to and telling jokes?
– chatting to people on buses?

Does she think these difficulties are mainly to do with language or mainly to do with culture?

3   Here are some expressions the woman uses. Find pairs (one from each
column) that she uses to make the same point. How does she use them?

Example She says that the new things she experiences abroad *stimulate* the
imagination and are *inspiring*.

stimulate	homesick
be assertive	on the outside
not integrated	exasperating
isolated	inspiring
frustrating	stand up for yourself

Now listen again and check your answers.

C   Impressions of Malaysia

You will hear a Scottish couple talking about
their experience of everyday life in Malaysia.
The recording is in two parts.

1   You will hear seven key sentences from
the first part of the recording.

What are the two people talking about?
What else do you think they are going to say?

Now listen to the first part of the recording.

2 Here are some words the speakers use about the markets in Malaysia. How are they connected? If necessary, listen to the recording again.

3 In the second part of the recording, the speakers talk about services in Malaysia. Listen and find answers to these questions:

1 Why do people listen to bananas?
2 Is Malaysia a good place to have clothes made?
3 What can you expect to happen at a Malaysian hairdresser's?

The woman repeats the word *pride* several times. What is the point she is making?
The man uses the expression *sell-by date*. What does this mean?

4 Which of these statements do you think reflect the speakers' attitude to living in Malaysia?

a) They found it exciting.
b) They found it frustrating.
c) They didn't try very hard to fit into the society.
d) Their attitude was different from most other foreigners.
e) They thought a lot of things were better than in Britain.

D Extension: Comparing experiences

1 In what ways were the experiences of the woman in Germany and the couple in Malaysia similar? In what ways were they different? Think about:

– the countries they were living in
– their lifestyles
– their attitude to living abroad

2 Look at the two lists you made in Section A. Were any of the things you noted down reflected in what you heard?

6 | The Louvre Pyramid

An opinion – and some alternatives

The Louvre before the Pyramid was built

The Louvre The Palais du Louvre stands at the heart of Paris, and houses one of the world's greatest collections of works of art. The original palace dates from 1527, and it was extended and added to over the next four centuries. It was first used as a public art gallery in 1793. In 1981, the Chinese-American architect Ieoh Ming Pei was commissioned to redevelop the public part of the Louvre and create more space for reception areas and services. He designed the famous Glass Pyramid, which serves as the main entrance to the building, leading underground to the museum and art gallery. The Pyramid is 21m high and 33m wide, and uses a combination of steel tubes, cables and sheet glass. It was completed in 1988, and quickly became a major tourist attraction in its own right.

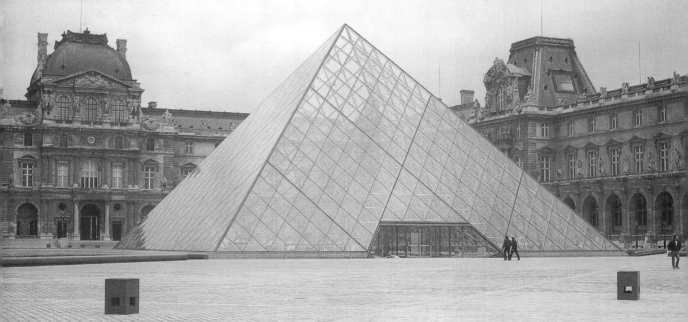

The Louvre Pyramid

A An architect's view

1   The pictures opposite show the Louvre in Paris as it used to be, and as it has looked since the Louvre Pyramid was built in 1988.

Look at the pictures and read the information about the Louvre Pyramid, then discuss these questions:

> Have any of you actually seen the Louvre Pyramid?
> What was your impression of it?
> Did you like it?

> What do you think the architect intended with this design?
> What would he have said about it?

Here are some opinions about the Pyramid. As far as you can judge from the pictures, which comments do you agree with?

A *It provides a focal point – people will come here specially to look at it.*

B *It's just a gimmick – in 50 years' time it will seem ridiculous, and will probably be pulled down.*

C *It's very arrogant to build something so modern right next to a great historic building.*

D *It's completely out of place – they should have built something that fits in better with the surrounding buildings.*

It's a building that demands your attention – you may love it or hate it, but you won't remain indifferent to it. E

F *It spoils the appearance of the square, and means it can't be used for anything else.*

G *It's interesting because it's so different from the Louvre itself.*

H *It's a lovely building – it conveys a feeling of light and beauty.*

2   ▭ You will hear an architect commenting on the Louvre Pyramid. Which of the opinions above would she agree with?

3   Here are some words the speaker uses. Do you know what they mean?

transparency   contrast
uninvolved   contradictory
complement   a lie

▭ Listen to the recording again.
What point is the speaker making when she uses each word?

B Watch this space

1 Imagine you are a committee considering alternatives to the Louvre
Pyramid. Here are three ideas. Look at each of them in turn, and decide
which you think is the best. Think about the following:

– visual interest
– harmony with the surroundings
– value to the community
– value as a tourist attraction
– probable cost

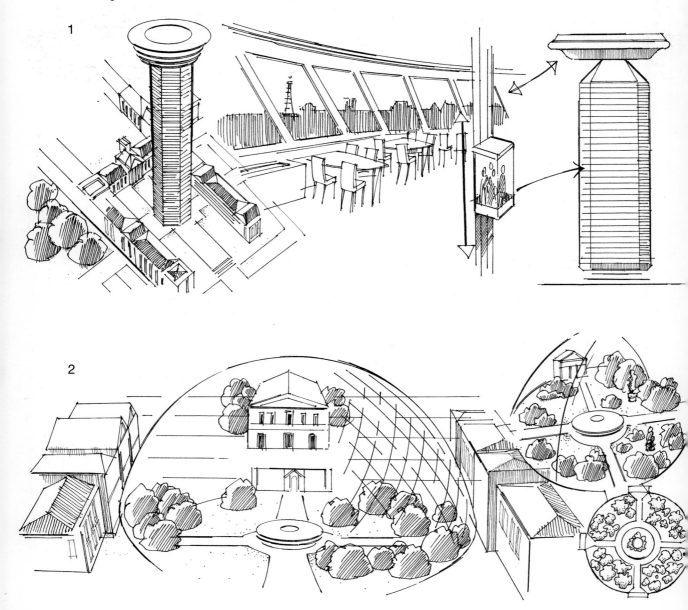

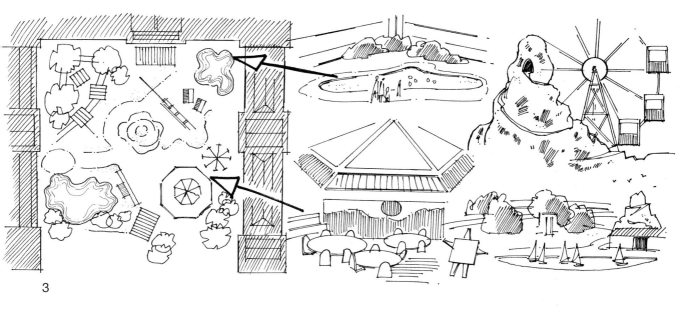

3

2   🔲 Listen to the three architects justifying their ideas.
Did they say anything that you hadn't already considered?

In the light of what they say, which idea do you think is the best?

C Extension: Design your own building

1   Together, choose a place with a large open space, either in your own area or
in another part of the world, and design an interesting building for it.

2   Present your idea to the rest of the class.

3   Take a class vote on the different ideas presented. (You can vote for any idea
except your own.)

7 | Technically speaking

Listening to technical explanations

A What's it about?

In this section you will hear three people giving technical explanations.

Part 1

1   You will hear someone giving an explanation which goes with this diagram.
What does the diagram show?
What kind of explanation do you think you will hear?

pancreas

2   [cassette] Listen to the first section of what the person says.
Write down four or five key words that you understood.
What do you think she is talking about?

[cassette] Now listen to the second section. Were you right?

3   [cassette] Listen again and complete this text:

The .... secretes ...., which you need to convert
.... into .... If you are a ...., the ....
stops working, so you have to ....; otherwise you will ....

Part 2

1   [cassette] You will hear someone describing a machine. The description is in
short sections. Every time the tape pauses, try to guess what the person is
talking about.

2   Listen again, and complete the instruction leaflet below.

How to make .... using your .... machine

1

2

3

4

5

Note   It is not necessary to .... the machine after use.

Part 3

📼 You will hear a description which includes these technical words:

a harness   a chock
to belay   a carabiner
rocks, friends, nuts and slings

Listen to the recording, which is in four sections. After each section, try to guess what the person is talking about, and what the technical words mean.

B Kite racing

1 Look at the picture. What direction is the man going in:

- downwind?
- across the wind?
- upwind?

2 You will hear a man describing the technique of kite racing. The recording is in two parts. Before you listen, read these questions:

1 What is a parakart?
2 What is a quadrafoil?
3 How fast can you go in a parakart?
4 Look at these three diagrams. Which shows a 'reach'? What do the other two show?
5 How do you stop a parakart?
6 What do you have to be careful about?

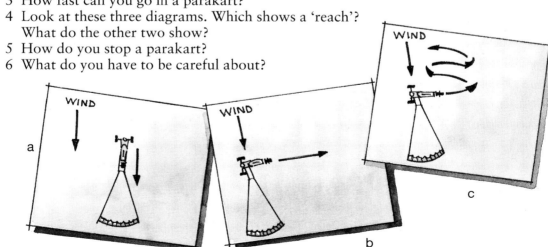

📼 Now listen to the whole recording once.
Can you answer the questions?

3   ⊡ The man talks with quite a strong French accent. Listen to the first part again, and spot these words as he says them:

and	lines	land-yachting
powered	miles an hour	sideways
parachute	principle	motion

Now see if this helps you answer Exercise 2 (questions 1–4).

4   ⊡ Listen to the second part again, and complete these sentences.

1 There's no .... on the kart, so you use the .... as a ....

2 If you .... quickly, the .... of the kart will make you ....

3 You have to be careful not to ...., and you have to anticipate that there may be ...., and make sure you ....

C Extension: Describing a process

1 Think of something you know about that other people may not know.
It could be:

- how you make something
- how something works
- how you use a piece of equipment

Make a few notes about it and look up any technical words you need in a dictionary.

2 Describe the process to other people in the class, and answer any questions they have.

8 | GWR FM

A day in the life of a local radio station

A On the air

1 Think of a local radio station in your area.

What kinds of things do they broadcast (e.g. music, local news …)?

Build up a list on the board.

2 ▭ You will hear nine items broadcast over a 24-hour period by GWR FM, a local radio station in England.

Listen to the items *once*, and try to catch what kind of items they are and roughly what they are about. After each one, jot down your answer in the table.

	What kind of item?	*What's it about?*
1	*Helping with listeners' problems*	
2		
3	*News broadcast*	*1* *2*
4		
5		
6		
7		
8		
9		

3   Work in groups. How much did you catch?
    How many of these questions can you answer?

Item 1
Whereabouts in the woman's house are the bees?
What does the presenter want bee-keeping listeners to do?

Item 2
How much could you save on a three-bedroom Persimmon house?
What are the words of the Persimmon jingle?

Item 3
By what time are rail travellers being advised to finish their journeys?
What is Inter City trying to arrange for tomorrow?
What did the policeman do to the boy?

Item 4
What will the weather be like tonight?
How hot was it earlier today?

Item 5
How do you win the game 'Record Recall'?
Can you name three of the artists featured on the twin-CD set?

Item 6
What did Elaine's dad decide to do himself? Why?

Item 7
What's surprising about the traffic today?
What's the traffic like in town?

Item 8
There were two questions about actors in films. Can you name the two films, the two actors, and the roles they played?
What was the final score?

Item 9
How far did Jeremy Bates get in the Manchester Open tournament?
What will be banned at Wimbledon this year?

▭ Now listen again for any answers you didn't get.

4   Look at these extracts from the recording. Can you explain the words in italics?

Item 3: A PC found himself *in the dock*.
Item 6: We're looking for the *daftest* thing your dad ever did.
Item 7: The trains of course are *out of action* today.
         Bumper to bumper around Templemeads and Old Market.
Item 8: Oh Ange. Thanks for *having a go*.

B A clip round the ear

1 In Section A, you heard a news item about a policeman called Steve Guscott. Fill the gaps in the story.

> POLICE OFFICER Steve Guscott was called after .... were tormenting .... He gave one teenager a ...., and the boy .... about it. PC Guscott has admitted .... at Bridgwater magistrates court. He could face .... and lose .... as a result of the incident.

Now listen to the news item again, and check your answers.

2 You will hear two further news items about the story which were broadcast on GWR FM the next morning.

What new information is given in each news item? Is there anything that contradicts what was said in the earlier report?

Massive support for P-c who slapped teenage troublemaker

DIXON IN THE DOCK
Yesterday's Page One

SACK HIM? HE'S A HERO

By Chris Rundle

A TIDAL wave of support poured in yesterday for P-c Steve Guscott who faces the sack after slapping a 14-year-old trouble-maker in the face.

West is braced for rail strike chaos

By Caroline Thomas

Overwhelmed ... P-c Steve Guscott relaxing yesterday

INSIDE Weather 2; Family Announcements 8; TV 12-13; Impressions 16-17; Gossip 17; Sunshine Club 18; Crossword 22; Sport 27-32

29

3   [cassette icon] Now listen to two stories told by listeners during a GWR FM phone-in that took place on the same day.

What is the theme of the phone-in?
Who clipped each speaker round the ear, and why?

Look at these opinions about the Guscott case. Which of them do you think the speakers would agree with?

A
The job of the police is to uphold the law. There's no room in the police force for officers who take the law into their own hands.

B
PC Guscott lost his head for a moment. He was wrong, but he should not have to pay for it with his career.

C
What exactly is the fuss about? A clip round the ear never did anyone any harm.

D
I have some sympathy with PC Guscott. But as a policeman, he must have known it was his job to prevent violence, not to indulge in it himself.

4   Which of the four opinions (if any) do you agree with?
What do you think should happen to PC Guscott?
(You can read what actually happened at the foot of this page.)

C   Extension activities

1   What impression do you get of GWR FM?
Would you tune into it regularly? sometimes? not at all?

2   Imagine you were in charge of GWR FM. What changes (if any) would you make to the programmes?

He kept his job after being given a reprimand.

9 | Loud and aggressive

One view of the music of the 90s

A From the 80s to the 90s

1 Look at the bands and singers in the pictures. Do you know anything about any of them?

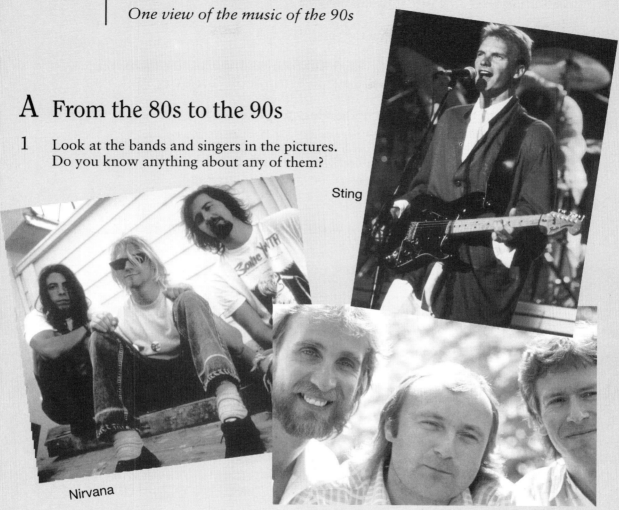

Sting

Nirvana

Genesis

2 ▭ You will hear Alex, a 22-year-old American, talking about how popular music changed from the 80s to the 90s. According to Alex, which of these adjectives apply more to 80s music, and which to 90s music?

loud	aggressive
tuneful	meaningful
serious	superficial
political	easy to listen to

3 Which of the singers in the pictures does Alex prefer, and why?

4 According to Alex, what caused the change between 80s and 90s music?

B *Low Self Opinion*

Alex now introduces the song *Low Self Opinion*, by the Henry Rollins Band. The recording is in three parts.

1 🔊 Listen to Alex introducing the song. What is it about?

2 🔊 You will hear part of the song. Listen and fill in the missing words on the opposite page. Play the recording more than once if necessary.

3 Now read the lyrics of the rest of the song. What do you like about the song? What don't you like about it?

4 🔊 Listen to the last part of the recording, in which Alex says what he likes about the song, and talks about the Henry Rollins Band.

How would he answer Question 3?

Did he say anything that helps you to understand or enjoy the song more?

C Extension: Personal choice

Is there a piece of music that's important to you at the moment?

Tell other students about it and say why you like it. If you can, bring it in and play it to them.

Low Self Opinion

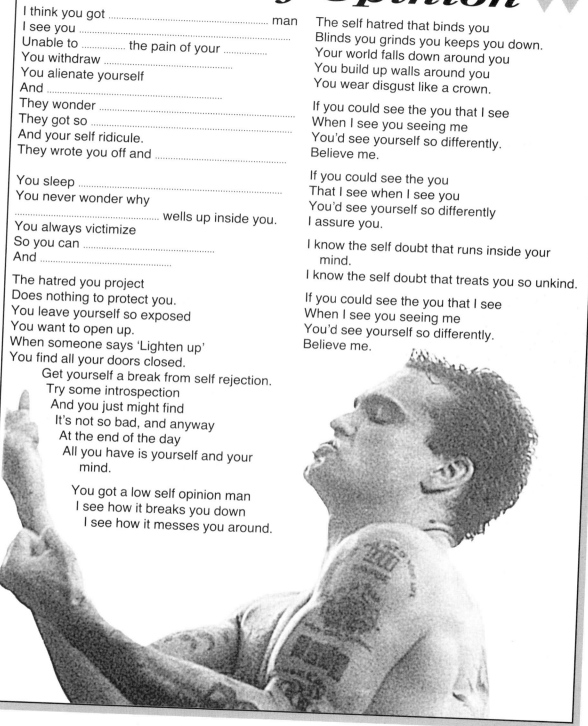

I think you got .... man
I see you ....
Unable to .... the pain of your ....
You withdraw ....
You alienate yourself
And ....
They wonder ....
They got so ....
And your self ridicule.
They wrote you off and ....

You sleep ....
You never wonder why
.... wells up inside you.
You always victimize
So you can ....
And ....

The hatred you project
Does nothing to protect you.
You leave yourself so exposed
You want to open up.
When someone says 'Lighten up'
You find all your doors closed.
     Get yourself a break from self rejection.
    Try some introspection
    And you just might find
     It's not so bad, and anyway
     At the end of the day
     All you have is yourself and your
      mind.

    You got a low self opinion man
    I see how it breaks you down
     I see how it messes you around.

The self hatred that binds you
Blinds you grinds you keeps you down.
Your world falls down around you
You build up walls around you
You wear disgust like a crown.

If you could see the you that I see
When I see you seeing me
You'd see yourself so differently.
Believe me.

If you could see the you
That I see when I see you
You'd see yourself so differently
I assure you.

I know the self doubt that runs inside your
  mind.
I know the self doubt that treats you so unkind.

If you could see the you that I see
When I see you seeing me
You'd see yourself so differently.
Believe me.

10 | Sarajevo

Three people talk about their experiences of war

A Under siege

1 In 1992–93 the city of Sarajevo was repeatedly bombarded, and almost completely cut off from the outside world.
Can you remember any particular things you read or heard about it at the time?

2 You will hear two women who lived through the bombardment describing what life was like. Before you listen, try to imagine how they lived and how they felt. Think of some questions you would like to ask them, and write them down.

3 ▭ Listen to the recording, which is in three parts.

Which of your questions did the women answer?
What answers did they give?

4 Judging from what the two women say, which of these characteristics do you think best describe the people of Sarajevo? Give examples from the recording.

courage	humour	pessimism	resourcefulness
anger	generosity	fatalism	greed

34

B Survival

1   One of the women goes on to describe how she survived the winter in Sarajevo.

Before you listen, try to imagine how you would keep warm and cook food. Discuss your ideas together. Talk about things you could do and things you couldn't do.

2   🔲 Listen to the recording.

What did she say that was similar to what you imagined?
What did she say that was different?

3   Here are some of the things she talks about:

furniture	tea	central heating
cardboard	her computer	a building site
bricks	chipboard	
a cushion	the fire escape	

How do all these elements fit together in her description?
If necessary, listen to the recording again.

C Leaving Sarajevo

1   ▣ You will hear a man describing his experience of leaving Sarajevo and going to Ljubljana in Slovenia. Listen to the recording.

How did he react to the things shown in the pictures? Why?

2   ▣ Listen again, and notice how the man expresses these ideas:

1 He was crying quietly to himself.
2 The villages hadn't been involved in the war.
3 I was surprised that Ljubljana was so prosperous.
4 The shops were full of things to buy.
5 The smell was wonderful.

What extra feeling is expressed by the words he uses? (e.g. Why does he say *weep* instead of *cry*?)

D Extension: Back in the 'real' world

Imagine that you have just left Sarajevo, like the three people you have heard. Which of these things would you want to do?

– go somewhere very quiet on your own
– visit lots of friends
– get in touch with other people who have been in Sarajevo
– tell people what it was like in Sarajevo
– try to forget all about it

What other things would you want to do?

11 | Out West

An American looks back on his family history

A Forefathers

1 You will hear an American describing how his family came to settle in Louisiana in the early 19th century. Before you listen, look at the map. Each number on the map shows a move that members of the family made.

📼 Listen to the first part, and note down the reason for each move.

2 📼 In the second part, the speaker goes on to talk about the American Civil War. Listen, and note down one or two things about:

– his three great great uncles
– the Tiger Regiment
– his great great uncle who was in the Tiger Regiment

Show your notes to someone else and compare them.

3 Did you catch all the details? How many of these questions can you answer?

   1 How long did the first Roberts spend as a prisoner?
   2 How many children did Silas Roberts have?
   3 How did they travel?
   4 Who was Sam Huston?
   5 Who looked after Silas's children when he went to war?
   6 How much money did he make from the war?
   7 How old are some of the graves in the Roberts cemetery?
   8 How did his great great uncle spend the last years of his life?
   9 How many Yankees had he killed?

   🔊 Listen to both parts of the recording again, and check your answers.

4 What kind of people do the speaker's ancestors seem to have been?
   How does he seem to feel about them?

B Great grandmother

In this Section, the speaker describes his great grandmother, and tells two stories about her.

1 🔊 Listen to the description just once. Then write down as many facts about the great grandmother as you can.
   Did you get them all?

2 The pictures show scenes from a story.

   What do you think the story is about?

   What do you think happens in picture D?

   🔊 Now listen to the story.

   How much did you get right?

3   You will hear the speaker describing how his great grandmother was alone on her farm when some bandits came by. From what you know about her, what do you imagine happened?

      Now listen to the story.

4   Here are some expressions the speaker used. What do they mean?

    1 a real pioneer woman
    2 a circuit-riding doctor
    3 a check-up
    4 the smoke-house
    5 they didn't stick around

C Extension activities

1   How far back can you remember your family history? Where did your ancestors come from? What did they do?

2   Imagine these pictures show two of your ancestors. Tell someone about them. Do you know any stories about either of them?

12 | Jigsaw of a village

Snapshots of life in an English village

A The pieces of the jigsaw

1 The people in these pictures all live in the village of Box in south-west England. What do you think their occupations are?

George & Jan

Dave

John

Julie

Philippe

Susan

2   📼 Work in two groups, A and B. Each group will need a cassette recorder. Listen only to your own part of the recording.

Working in your groups, decide which of the people you are listening to and note down the main points you understand in the table below. You will only be able to complete half the table. Listen more than once if you need to.

	What's their occupation, and what do they say about it?	What happens in the scene you heard from their work?
 Philippe		
 Susan		
 Julie		
 George & Jan		
 Dave		
 John		

Group A

You will hear people from five of the pictures:

– three recorded at work
– two talking about their work

Group B

You will hear people from five of the pictures:

– two recorded at work
– three talking about their work

3   Form pairs – one person from Group A and one person from Group B. Tell each other what you found out about each person, and write brief notes in your table.

Two of the boxes should remain empty. Which ones are they?

4   Stay in your pairs. Did you catch the details? Working together, write
     answers to the questions below.

     1 Who came to the village last year?
     2 What can be plain or cheese and onion?
     3 What would you do with a half of 6X?
     4 Which of these things does the butcher make himself?
        – bacon   – sausages
        – cheese   – pies
     5 What does the publican say about
        – Kiwis?   – the navy?   – a parrot?
     6 Is the vicar married or single?
     7 Is the school getting bigger or smaller?
     8 What kind of wine do the people in the restaurant order?
     9 Which letters are the children practising?
    10 Why are the schoolgirls studying Austria and France?

    Which pair had the most correct answers?

B Living in Box

1   You will hear five of the people saying what they think of the village as
     a place to live. What do they say about:

     – facilities for children?
     – facilities for adults?
     – things going on in the village?
     – the appearance of the village?
     – the people who live in the village?

2   Imagine you went to live in Box. What do you think you would like most
     about it? Is there anything that you wouldn't like about it?

C Extension: Village profile

     Imagine you are writing an article about Box village for a magazine, which
     includes a paragraph about each of the five people you heard in the
     recording.

     Use your notes to write about one of them, inventing any details you like.

13 | All you need is love?

Two views of relationships and marriage

A A partner for life

1   Which of these things do you think are important in making a relationship succeed? Give each one a score from 5 (very important) to 0 (not at all important).

Physical attraction ☐

Similar sense of humour ☐

Ability to go through bad times together ☐

Being able to give and take ☐

Similar interests ☐

Being able to talk to each other ☐

Similar social background ☐

Having enough money ☐

Similar attitudes and opinions ☐

Clearly defined roles ☐

Being in love ☐

Compare your scores with other students. How many points did you agree on?

2   [cassette] You will hear someone talking about relationships.

Which of the points in the list does she mention?
What score do you think she would give for each?

3   What impression do you have of the speaker? Only one of these descriptions of the speaker is true. Which do you think it is? Why?

a) She's in her mid 20s. She has had several boyfriends, but has never wanted to get married. She met her present boyfriend six months ago.

b) She's in her early 40s, and married. She met her husband 23 years ago, when they were students at university. They have no children.

c) She's in her late 30s. She was married for ten years, and then separated. She has been living on her own for the last two years.

d) She's in her late 40s. She has been married for 26 years, and has four teenage children.

4   What exactly is the point she is making about:
- physical appearance?
- the divorce rate in Britain?
- novels by Barbara Cartland?
- falling in love?

Imagine you were able to talk to the speaker. What would you say to her about each of these points?

B An arranged marriage

In this Section, you will hear an interview with a member of the Sikh community in Britain, who talks about the idea of arranged marriage.

1   Before you listen, discuss what you already know about arranged marriages. What actually happens? How does the system work?

2   📼 Listen to the first part of the interview. Which of these statements represent what the speaker says?

    a) He and his wife were childhood friends.
    b) He and his wife were both equally happy to get married.
    c) Once the parents have chosen a partner, the children usually have to accept it.
    d) Sometimes it is the children who choose who they would like to marry.
    e) His wife's mother took the first steps in arranging their marriage.
    f) He and his wife have similar interests and opinions.
    g) Their marriage has been a success.
    h) Money is a very important consideration in choosing a husband.

3   In view of what the speaker has said so far, write down any questions you would like to ask him about arranged marriages.

    Show your questions to other students.

    What do you imagine the speaker would say in reply?

4   📼 Listen to the second part of the interview.

    Did the speaker answer any of your questions?

    Look at the list in Section A. What scores do you think the speaker would give for each item?

5   What exactly is the point he is making about:

    – marriage and educational courses?
    – the role of the parents?
    – love?

    Imagine you were able to talk to the speaker. What would you say to him about each of these points?

C Extension: Do you still think the same?

Look back at the scores you gave in Section A.

Have you heard anything (in the recordings or in your own discussions) that makes you want to change any of your scores?

14 | Get it?

Children's jokes and classic comedy

A Children's jokes

1 Have you heard any of these jokes before?

🔊 If not, listen to each one being told and write in the punch-line.

What's the joke?

Q
What time is it when an elephant sits on your fence?

A ....

Q Why did the owl 'owl?

A ....

Q Why did the chicken cross the road?

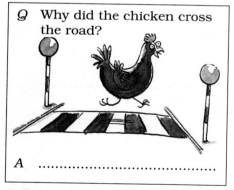

A ....

THIRTY YEARS
in the SADDLE
by MAJOR ....

– Knock knock
– Who's there?
– Lena.
– Lena who?
– ....

Girl: I wish we lived in the olden days.
Teacher: Why?
Girl: ....

2 Match these joke beginnings with the endings in the box.

1 Why was six afraid of seven?
2 – Knock knock (Who's there?)
   – Boo (Boo who?)
3 Why did the chewing gum cross the road?
4 Why did the duck cross the road?
5 Why did the dinosaur cross the road?
6 Why did the fly fly?
7 When were there only three vowels?
8 What did the policeman say to his tummy?
9 – Knock knock (Who's there?)
   – Isabel (Isabel who?)
10 Have you read 'How to Save Money'
11 What do you call a deer with no eyes?

a) Isabel necessary on a bicycle?
b) by Iona Fortune?
c) It was the chicken's day off.
d) You're under a vest.
e) Because seven eight nine.
f) Because the spider spider.
g) Chickens weren't invented yet.
h) There's no need to cry – it's only a joke.
i) No idea.
j) It was stuck to the chicken's leg.
k) Before you and I were born.

Now listen and check your answers. Which of the jokes did you 'get'?

3 You will hear three jokes which tell stories. Listen to each joke, and decide how funny it is. Give it a score out of five.

Joke 1 *Score:*

Joke 2 *Score:*

Joke 3 *Score:*

B *The Bricklayer*

In 1958, British musician and comedian Gerard Hoffnung recorded a performance at Oxford University. You will hear a monologue from the performance.

1   Listen to the introduction.

– Who wrote a letter? Who did he write it to?

– '... keeping the upper lip stiff'. Does this mean:
a) talking in a strange way?
b) making a lot of fuss over nothing?
c) being brave when suffering?

2   Read the first part of the letter. Mark the points where you would expect the audience to laugh.

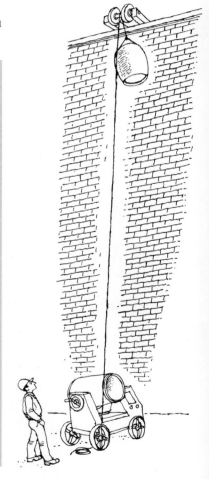

> Respected sir,
>
>   When I got to the top of the building I found that the hurricane had knocked some bricks off the top. So I rigged up a beam with a pulley at the top of the building and hoisted up a couple of barrels full of bricks. When I had fixed the building there was a lot of bricks left over. I hoisted the barrel back up again and secured the line at the bottom and then went up and filled the barrel with extra bricks. Then I went to the bottom and cast off the line. Unfortunately, the barrel of bricks was heavier than I was, and before I knew what was happening the barrel started down, jerking me off the ground. I decided to hang on, and halfway up I met the barrel coming down, and received a severe blow on the shoulder.

   Now listen to the first part of the letter.
At which points did the audience laugh? Why?

3   You will hear the rest of the letter. Each time the audience laughs, try to predict what will happen next.

4   In your opinion, what does the humour of the monologue depend on?
    How important are:

    – the story itself?
    – the way the letter is read?
    – the style in which the letter is written?

5   In Britain, *The Bricklayer* is widely regarded as a classic piece of comedy.
    How do you react to it? Do you agree with any of the following?

    a) It's very funny.
    b) You need to be a native speaker to appreciate it fully.
    c) It must have been very funny once, but now it seems a bit old-fashioned.
    d) If this is British humour, they can keep it!

C Extension: Making people laugh

Do you know any English-language jokes? Or any jokes that translate into
English?

Try to make other people in the class laugh.

15 | In black and white (1)

An artist talks about print-making techniques

A Four techniques

You will hear part of an illustrated lecture by Dutch artist Nan Mulder about different ways of making prints.

1   Before you listen, look at the four prints on pages 52–53.
    Do you know which is
    – an etching?   – an engraving?
    – a mezzotint?   – a woodcut?

2   Look at these pieces of equipment. Which do you think are used for which technique? How do you think they are used?

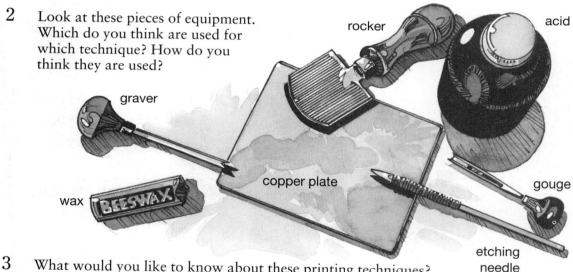

3   What would you like to know about these printing techniques? Write down one or two questions.

B The lecture (Part 1)

1   [cassette] Listen to the first part of the lecture, which describes two of the techniques. For each description, make brief notes under these headings:

Name of technique
Equipment
How is it done?

2 Judging from the pictures and from what the speaker says, which technique do you think is:

– older?
– easier?
– more versatile?

C The lecture (Part 2)

1 ▭ Listen to the artist describing the third technique. Make notes under these headings:

Name of technique	
Differences from first two techniques	1 2
Ways of recognising the technique	1 2

2 Here are the lecturer's notes about the last technique. Read them through.

3 ▭ Now listen to the last part of the lecture.

What information is in the notes, but not in the lecture?
What information is in the lecture, but not in the notes?

> Mezzotint
>
> Technique invented by Jan Blom, 1710.
> ('mezzo tinto' = medium shade)
> Not a common technique nowadays.
> Tools — copper plate (hard), rocker (tiny points)
> Technique: rock over plate → tiny holes → black.
> 'Burr' beside holes:
> – put back in holes or scrape off.
> → different shades, from dark to light.
> More work = lighter (like woodcut).

D Extension: Your own questions

Look at the questions you wrote in Section A.
Which of them were answered in the lecture?

Read out the questions that weren't answered. See if anyone else in the class can answer them.

1 *End-of-year Festival*, by Hans Sebald Beham, 1546

2 *Homestead*, by Patrick Pye, 1989

3 *Lida at the table*,
by Herman Gordijn, 1984

4 *After a painting by
Joshua Reynolds*, by
James McArdell, 1756

53

16 | In black and white (2)

Frame Story II: *a modern mezzotint*

A *Frame Story II*

Frame Story II, by Nan Mulder, 1976

1   Look at the picture. What do you think the 'story' is?
Consider these elements in the picture:

the house	the cat	the couple
the curtains	the letter	the path
the birds	the landscape	

2 Which of these adjectives do you think best describe the house and the landscape beyond it? Are there any other adjectives you would choose to describe them?

deserted   wild   cosy   romantic
peaceful   sad   abandoned   mysterious

3 What (if anything) do you like about the picture?
   Is there anything you don't like about it?

4 ⊡ You will hear a woman saying what she thinks about the picture. How would she answer the questions above?

B The artist's version

1 Nan Mulder studied mezzotint in Poland, then worked as an artist in Amsterdam. She later visited Scotland, where she met her future husband, and shortly afterwards produced this mezzotint.

Can you find elements in the picture that might refer to these events in her life?

2 ⊡ Listen to her description of the picture. How, according to her, do the elements in the picture fit together to make a story of her life?

Does she say anything that agrees with the woman's interpretation in Section A?

C Interpreting a picture

You have considered several different interpretations of *Frame Story II*: your own, the woman's in Section A and the artist's own explanation. What conclusions do you come to from this? Which of these statements do you agree with?

A *Pictures can mean anything you want them to mean — interpreting them is just a kind of game.*

B *To understand a picture properly, you really need to know something about the artist and what he/she intended — otherwise you can't appreciate it.*

C *A good picture contains all kinds of different meanings, and it can say different things to different people. All that's important is what it means to you.*

D *Artists often don't understand their own work, and what they say about their own pictures may not be very important.*

E *A good picture is like a mirror — what we see in it says more about us than about the picture itself.*

D Extension: The making of *Frame Story II*

1 In Unit 15, you heard Nan describe how mezzotints are made.
What can you remember of what she says about the technique?

2 From what you know about mezzotints, try to guess the answers
to these questions:

1 How long did it take Nan to prepare the copper plate for *Frame Story II*?
2 How long did it take to make the picture itself?
3 Which parts of the picture took longest to do?
4 Which parts took the least time to do?
5 Why did Nan give up making mezzotints?

Now listen to Nan talking about how she produced *Frame Story II*.
How good were your guesses?

17 | *The Great Ruby Robbery* (1)

A radio drama based on a Victorian detective story

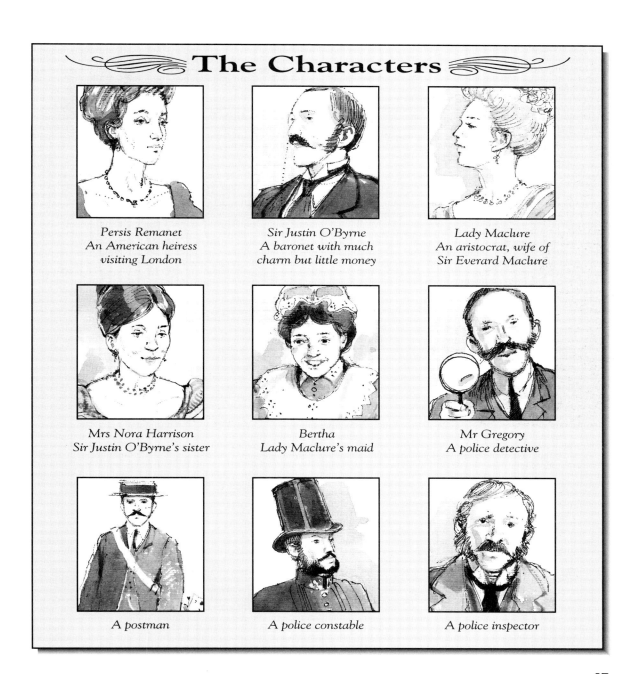

The Characters

Persis Remanet
*An American heiress
visiting London*

Sir Justin O'Byrne
*A baronet with much
charm but little money*

Lady Maclure
*An aristocrat, wife of
Sir Everard Maclure*

Mrs Nora Harrison
Sir Justin O'Byrne's sister

Bertha
Lady Maclure's maid

Mr Gregory
A police detective

A postman

A police constable

A police inspector

A The opening scene

It is nearly two o'clock in the morning on a warm summer's night in London. Persis Remanet has been to a ball, and is now on her way back to the house of Sir Everard and Lady Maclure, with whom she is staying as a guest. She is accompanied by her friends Nora Harrison and Sir Justin O'Byrne …

1 ▭ Listen to Scene 1 of *The Great Ruby Robbery*. As you listen, consider these questions:

1 Where are the rubies?
2 What is Persis going to do next week?
3 Why does Sir Justin want to marry her?
4 Why doesn't he want to marry her?
5 How does Persis feel about it?

2 Here are some expressions the speakers use. Who uses them? What do they mean by them? If necessary, listen to them again in context.

That might do for an Englishman, but it won't do for me.

I could snap my fingers at them.

I'm a man about town.

a regular fortune-hunter

Reminds one of Romeo and Juliet.

3 What do you imagine will be the next development in the plot?

B The plot thickens

Listen to Scenes 2–4 . After each scene, answer the questions.

Scene 2

1 What do we know about:

– the rubies?   – the jewel case?
– the door?   – Bertha, the maid?
– the window?

2 What different explanations can you think of for what happened?
Build up a list on the board. Which one seems most likely?

Scene 3

1 Here are three of Mr Gregory's theories about crime. Can you complete them?

1 People often think something has been stolen, but in fact they've …
2 If people are sure they put something away safely, it usually …
3 The person who committed the robbery is usually …

2 Look at your list of explanations. Do any of them now seem more or less likely? Are there any other possibilities?

Scene 4

1 Complete the table.

Reasons to suspect Sir Justin O'Byrne
1
2
3

2 Here are some expressions used in the scene. Match the two halves together.

blameless   crime
despicable   in his clothes
delicate   for a burglary
entangled   character
convenient   matter

Which speaker used each expression? What did he/she say?

3 Do you suspect Sir Justin O'Byrne?

18 | *The Great Ruby Robbery (2)*

A radio drama based on a Victorian detective story

A The story so far

> Persis Remanet's rubies have disappeared, and Mr Gregory has been called in to investigate the crime …

1 What do we know so far about:

   – the rubies?   – Sir Justin O'Byrne?   – Bertha?
   – Persis?   – Lady Maclure?   – Mr Gregory?

2 Which person or people do you suspect most strongly? Why?

B The story continues

Listen to Scenes 5–11. After each scene, discuss these questions.

1 Which picture goes with the scene you have just heard? What does it show?

2 What have we found out so far that might be important?
Who do you suspect? Why?

C The solution

🔊 The last scene is in two parts. Listen to the first part.

Who is the inspector talking about?
How do you think the crime was committed?
How do you think the crime was solved?

🔊 Now listen to the second part. Were you right?

D Happy ending

Imagine an ending to the story. What do you think happened to:

– Persis Remanet?   – Mr Gregory?
– Sir Justin O'Byrne?   – Bertha?

🔊 Now listen to the last paragraph of the original story, as it appeared in the *Strand Magazine* in 1892.

19 | Family life (2)

A mother and her teenage daughter discuss conflicts between them

A House rules

1   Think about the time when you were a young teenager (14–16 years old). If you are 14–16 now, or if you have children of that age, think about your present situation.

Which of these things caused conflict between you and your parents?
What exactly were the conflicts about?
Who do you think was right?

Keeping your room tidy

Getting up
in the morning

Watching television

Going out with
your friends

Staying
out late

2 ▭ You will hear a mother and her 14-year-old daughter commenting in
   turn on each topic. The recording is in five sections. After each section, note
   down the speakers'
   different points of view
   in the table.

	Mother	Daughter
Keeping her room tidy		
Getting up in the morning		
Watching television		
Going up to London		
Staying out late		

3 Look at these statements about the daughter. Which are true and which are
   false? What did you hear that makes you think so?

   1 She's an only child.
   2 She enjoys soap operas.
   3 She's learning the piano and the violin.
   4 She often wears make-up.
   5 She's not doing very well at school.
   6 Most of her friends have stricter parents than she does.

4 Here are some expressions the mother and daughter use. What do they mean?

   1 I'm not a morning person.
   2 She sneaks in a fair amount more than that.
   3 ... as streetwise as they think they are ...
   4 ... they might get mugged.
   5 There's safety in numbers

5 Consider each of the topics again. Do you think the mother is:

   – too strict?   – not strict enough?   – about right?

   How does she compare with your own parents (or with yourself as a parent?)

B State school or private school?

1   Read this text about school education in Britain. What reasons do you think parents might have for sending their child to:

   – the local comprehensive school?
   – an expensive private school?

2   Louisa is at a comprehensive school, but her parents are planning to send her to a private school next year.

   [cassette icon] Look at these opinions about state and private education, and then listen to Louisa and her mother talking. Which opinions does the mother seem to hold? Which does the daughter seem to hold? Are there any opinions they seem uncertain or confused about?

> ## School education in Britain
>
> In Britain, there are two parallel education systems – state schools and private schools.
>
> Most people send their children to state schools, which are free, and usually this means going to the local comprehensive school.
>
> Comprehensive schools are generally fairly large, and take children of all interests and abilities.
>
> Some parents choose instead to send their children to private schools, which charge school fees and require the child to pass an entrance test.
>
> Nearly all comprehensive schools take both boys and girls, whereas many private schools are single-sex.

a) People send their children to private schools out of snobbery.
b) Private schools give you a better all-round education.
c) Mixed education is better than single-sex education.
d) Single-sex education produces better results.
e) Private schools encourage you to work harder.
f) Private schools are better for extra-curricular subjects (e.g. music).
g) You come into contact with a wider range of people at a state school.
h) State schools prepare you better for the real world.

3   Discuss these questions:

Do you think Louisa's mother really believes private schools are better, or does she just want to 'look good in front of other people'?
Do you think Louisa really accepts that private school would be better, or is she just going there to please her parents?
Imagine you were Louisa's mother or father, and had enough money to send her to a private school. What would you do?

C Extension: Role play

> *Student A* You are Louisa's mother or father. You want to send her to a private school. Try to convince her that it would be a good idea.

> *Student B* You are Louisa. You would really rather stay at your local comprehensive school. Try to convince your mother/father that it would be better.

20 | *Here*

A woman talks about a poem by Philip Larkin

Here

Swerving east, from rich industrial shadows
And traffic all night north; swerving through fields
Too thin and thistled to be called meadows,
And now and then a harsh-named halt, that shields   *halt* = a small station
5   Workmen at dawn; swerving to solitude
Of skies and scarecrows, haystacks, hares and pheasants,
And the widening river's slow presence,
The piled gold clouds, the shining gull-marked mud,   *gull* = a seabird

Gathers to the surprise of a large town:
10 Here domes and statues, spires and cranes cluster
Beside grain-scattered streets, barge-crowded water,   *barge* = a flat boat for
And residents from raw estates, brought down   carrying goods
The dead straight miles by stealing flat-faced trolleys,   *stealing* = moving silently
Push through plate-glass swing doors to their desires –   *trolleys* = trolley-buses
15 Cheap suits, red kitchen-ware, sharp shoes, iced lollies,
Electric mixers, toasters, washers, driers –

A cut-price crowd, urban yet simple, dwelling
Where only salesmen and relations come
Within a terminate and fishy-smelling   *terminate* = at the end of
20 Pastoral of ships up streets, the slave museum,   a railway line
Tattoo-shops, consulates, grim head-scarved wives;   *pastoral* = a scene
And out beyond its mortgaged half-built edges   *mortgaged* (of houses) =
Fast-shadowed wheat-fields, running high as hedges,   bought with borrowed
Isolate villages, where removed lives   money

25 Loneliness clarifies. Here silence stands
Like heat. Here leaves unnoticed thicken,
Hidden weeds flower, neglected waters quicken,
Luminously-peopled air ascends;
And past the poppies bluish neutral distance
30 Ends the land suddenly beyond a beach
Of shapes and shingle. Here is unfenced existence:
Facing the sun, untalkative, out of reach.

A The poem

1   Read the poem, which describes a train journey to the north-east of
England. Don't expect to understand everything straight away.

As you read through it, underline any unfamiliar words that really seem
important to help you understand the poem. Look them up in a dictionary.

2   ▭ Now listen to the poem being read.

Look at the pictures.
Which lines of the poem do you think they go with?

3   What feeling does the poem give you about:

– the landscape in Verse 1?
– the town in Verses 2 and 3?
– the landscape in Verse 4?

C

D

E

F

G

67

B An interpretation

In this Section, a woman talks about the poem, and then goes on to say how she feels about the north-east of England.

1 ▭ Listen to the first part of the recording.

What does she say that matches what you thought about the poem? Does she say anything that you didn't realise about the poem or which surprises you?

2 Which of the scenes in the pictures on pages 66–67 does she describe? What does she say about them?

3 From what she has said so far, what do you think her feelings are about this part of England?

    a) She hates it, and is glad to have left.
    b) She misses it greatly and is longing to return.
    c) She has mixed feelings about it – she's glad not to live there any more, but she feels nostalgic about it.

    ▭ Now listen to the second part of the recording. Were you right?

4 She uses a number of words that describe the atmosphere and mentality of the people in this part of England. Note them down in two lists:

    Positive: open, …
    Negative: provincial, …

C Extension: Going home

1 Have you moved from the town or village where you grew up?
Do you miss it?
Are you glad you moved away?
What do you feel when you go back?

2 Imagine you're taking a train journey home.

What do you see through the window?
Note down some words and phrases that come to mind.

Read out what you have written to another student.

Tapescript

Unit 1   I was scared to death

1A   *Dracula*

EXERCISE 2

5 May. My first impression of Count Dracula is as vivid as ever. It was within minutes of midnight. As we approached the ruined castle, a dog began to howl somewhere far down the road, a long, agonised wailing. The horses shivered. A louder and sharper howling of wolves began. I was afraid to speak or move. The coach was entering the courtyard of Count Dracula's castle. I heard the sound of rattling chains and the clanking of massive bolts drawn back. 'Welcome to my house. You may go anywhere you wish in my castle, but never attempt to unlock certain rooms.' He was clad in black from head to foot. The Count's face was strong, aquiline, with a domed forehead. His mouth under a heavy moustache rather cruel, the teeth peculiarly sharp. His ears were pale and pointed, and his breath was rank. A horrible nausea came over me.

EXERCISE 3

8 May. I had just begun to shave when I heard the Count's voice wishing me a good morning. He was close to me, and I could see him over my shoulder. But there was no reflection of him in the mirror. I cut myself and the blood trickled over my chin. With a demoniac fury, he made a grab at my throat. His fingers touched the crucifix, given to me by an old lady on my arrival in the country. The fury passed away so quickly, I could hardly believe that it had been. I breakfasted alone. I have not seen the Count eat or drink. I wonder why. The castle is on the edge of a terrible precipice. Here and there are silver threads, where the rivers wind in deep gorges through the forests. The castle is a veritable prison, and I am a prisoner.

12 May. I saw Count Dracula slowly emerging from the window of his bedchamber. He began to crawl down the castle wall over that dreadful abyss face down, his cloak spreading out around him like great wings. There was a dread loneliness in the place which chilled my heart and made my nerves tremble.

1B   *The Vanishing*

EXERCISE 1

One film I did find really horrific was *The Vanishing* by George Sluizer. It was a French/Dutch film and it was set in France. It's about a young couple who are on a holiday in France, and the girl disappears. Her boyfriend doesn't know what happened to her, she just walked into a petrol station and then never came back. The audience knows what happened to her, she was abducted by a sicko who killed her. He put her in a coffin underground and let her die, she was alive in the coffin. Meanwhile he and his family were romping and frolicking and picnicking above ground, and he was very conscious of what had happened and what he'd done. He was just a really sick man. And most of the story is about the boyfriend's obsessive search for his girlfriend, he desperately desperately wants to know what happened to her. And three years after his girlfriend disappeared he encounters the murderer. He knows that this is the person who had something to do with her disappearance. And so he goes with the murderer back to France and meets the same fate as his girlfriend, in fact. He's drugged, he – and this is the final scene of the film, this is what is so horrifying about it. First of all you see him being drugged, and then the next thing you see is this boy lying in a coffin lighting his lighter, realising where he is, and going 'Oh no.' And because it's done in such a low-key matter-of-fact way it's totally believable and totally chilling. It's just one of the most horrible fates you can imagine, and it gave me the creeps for weeks afterwards.

1C   *Why do people watch horror films?*

EXERCISE 2

A: Now we're going to discuss the horror genre, the horror movie. Now what is it, do you think, that makes us want to pay £5.50 to sit in a draughty cinema and have ourselves terrified or spooked? What is that?

B: I don't know, I mean I've loved going ever since I was a kid, and it was 50 cents rather than £5 or $10 or whatever. I just love being scared.

C: Yes, I think the element of suspense (Yeah).

A: I think probably too, I don't know, you know maybe we all have some really deep-rooted fear that we can't deal with, and perhaps by going to see a movie that has that fear in it, you know, maybe being trapped or fear of the dark or something, in some sort of way it helps you to deal with it as well. Because you're not actually experiencing it and yet it's helping you (Yes) cope with it yourself.

C: It actually makes you feel more secure as a person.

B: Do you think there's an element of voyeurism in it, in that, the way you might slow down at a road accident and look, everybody does that.

D: Yes (I think you're right). Well I mean I think that's something within us all, isn't it? I mean it's …

A: Yes, you only have to look at the tabloids to see.

D: Yeah, I mean it's something really gruesome happening to somebody else (To somebody else) (That's right, yes) and yeah, thank heavens it's not happening to me.

C: And part of you doesn't want to look at it and yet there's part of you that does (Yes). You can't sort of keep away (Yes) …

A: … And also I think some of the, you know the really old ones, well not necessarily the old ones, but ones with, like Vincent Price (Bela Lugosi), they're just so entertaining (Oh yes) and really funny a lot of the time.

C: They kept to a very simple formula then (Oh yeah, yes), didn't they?

A: Yes, great movies. I think part of the enjoyment was that you knew what was going to happen (Yes) (Sure, yes), and you enjoyed the unravelling of the plot. It was a shared experience …

Unit 2   Family life (1)

2A   The perfect parent

EXERCISE 2

1 I think parents shouldn't push a particular narrow point of view or morality on children. For example, religion. I think they should even if they hold a very strong religious point of view themselves that they should allow the child room to develop herself in that area. And I think they should encourage questioning of authority as far as possible, parental authority as well. As a child I didn't like being told 'You have to do this because I'm your mother or father and I say so.' I think that's a bit of a cop-out really. I think I would have liked to have seen reasons behind what was being asked of me. Looking back now, what I don't like so much was the strength of their religious beliefs and the way that they expected the children to share their beliefs. My parents were actually missionaries in India for five years, and my Dad worked as a doctor in a hospital there. At the time I didn't mind at all going to church every Sunday, going to Sunday school, grace before every meal, but it did lead to a rather strict disciplinary code in their way of bringing us up, and looking back now I feel like I would have had a much sort of richer childhood if we hadn't been pushed into this kind of narrow way of thinking. I think I would have had a much wider range of experiences. And I think it's led to a lack of communication with my parents which still hasn't been overcome, because all of our children have developed such a different lifestyle to my parents' lifestyle, and there's quite a lack of common ground, which causes communication problems, yeah.

2 My parents gave me a lot of free time. After dinner, during the week when I was say even 15 years old they would let me go out until ten o'clock and they would never ask where I went. I would smoke cigarettes and drink beer, at 15 years old I would hang out in the local pubs and these were type of things that I don't think were too good for me at that time. I think my parents should have maybe at least showed an interest as to where I was going. They never even asked where I was going and they they gave me a lot of free time, and I think that they felt that this was a thing that was being a good parent. But I think that teenagers are very naive, and I was as a teenager very naive, and I think I could have used a little more direction from them. These days a lot of parents think they should be lenient with their children, they should let them grow and experience on their own. I think that's what my parents were doing, I think there's a Biblical saying 'Spare the rod, spoil the child' and I think that really applies. And I think you need to direct especially young people. They can be thrown into such a harsh world, especially if you live in a city. I lived in a very small village and it was still a very rough crowd that I found in that village. And my parents never asked questions, and if they only knew they would be shocked.

2B   Brothers and sisters

EXERCISE 2

Roger

Being one of nine, I, I grew up in a very crowded situation. We – materially we didn't have too much, but we had a lot in our sort of day-to-day life at home, with the family unit. We had good times at home, very few bad times as I can remember – being disciplined I suppose when I reached the age of 11, 10–11, beginning to sort of you know get a bit arrogant, so my father had to deal with me once or twice. But those years, the childhood years, were as far as I'm concerned probably the best of my life to date. I enjoyed being with my brothers and sisters. We had lots of fun and lots of laughs – we still laugh when we get together. And it's funny now, growing up in a house, and a crowded house where I always had a brother or sometimes two brothers sharing a room, I like my privacy now. Whereas being at home I couldn't get that, and I do treasure my privacy now, I sort of crave it, you know when I can get in a little corner and not get disturbed etcetera, I do like that now.

Tasia

Well I was the younger sister in my family, there were two of us, my older sister and myself. And it was a very nice relationship, I guess, my sister used to look after me very … very well. And we weren't only, there wasn't only the two of us, there were also another three, another two boys another girl who my mum brought up. And I was the youngest of all these children in the family, and I was very well looked after, very spoilt by them. I could play in all their games, I was never left out. And the only disadvantage of being the youngest was that I got all the leftovers, all the clothes, all the old shoes, all … And very rarely was it where I went out to the shops you know to get something new. I had to wear all the leftovers, and that wasn't something that I very much enjoyed … And – but elsewise I was … I was quite spoilt actually. I mean all the rest of them used to get into trouble, I never used to get into trouble. They used to get spanked, I never used to get spanked, so I used to, not enjoy it, but I used to get away with a lot of things, I could do a lot of things and get away with them whereas all the rest they couldn't do anything and get away with it.

Hazel

I was a third child in a family of four children. I had an older brother and sister and a younger sister. And as number three I was never quite sure of my role in the family. I wasn't the first-born, and I wasn't the longed-for boy, and I wasn't the baby of the family, so I felt quite out of it a lot of the time. My brother and sister were quite intelligent, musical, my brother was very good at sports, and again when I was quite young I always felt there was nothing that I could do that was better than they could do. If I had my time again I think I would like to be the first-born, but definitely not the only child, because the advantages of brothers and sisters I think far outweigh the disadvantages. Having an older brother and sister meant that I was never alone, so there was a great lack of privacy on the down side, but as a plus you were never alone, you always had somebody to play with, and even if you had rowed with one there was always somebody else that you could play with.

Chris

Yeah, well I was I'm an only child, and there was just me and my parents and my grandparents living at home. Well I think in many ways it was a very good experience and in many ways it wasn't. The good thing was obviously that, at the time at least, was that I was at the centre of everything and so everybody always had time for me, I never had to wait, I was never in line with other brothers and sisters. I was able to learn quickly, and I got lots of attention and lots of help with anything that I wanted.

The down side of it I suppose was that I was a bit isolated. I mean with my own children I notice that they're never bored because they play with each other all the time if there's nobody else around. But if I wanted to actually play with other kids I had to get out of the house, go next door and see if somebody was free or whether somebody could come out to play, all this kind of thing. So it was a little bit lonesome in some ways. And I think now thinking of my adult life, I think, I think in some ways you know I'm a very private person, I like to have my own space around me, I never learnt that I had to kind of share everything I had, and that my space wasn't my own. And I find having personal space around me where I can be completely alone I find very very important. And I think that's probably because I spent such a long time alone when I was a child.

Unit 3   The sound of selling

3A   *Catchy tunes*

[Three tunes played on an electronic keyboard]

3B   *At the keyboard*

EXERCISE 1

Part 1

A: So Graham, you write music for television commercials (That's right). Why do they have music in television commercials? What's it for? What's its purpose?

B: Well, sometimes it sets the mood or illustrates the action that's on the screen. Other times it can be background for someone speaking, someone describing the product. For example, for a newspaper I might write something like this [plays] and the person would be saying 'Tomorrow in the Sunday Globe – Is the Prime Minister an alien?' or something like that. Or it could be just a jingle.

A: Jingle?

B: A jingle is a song with the name of the product in it. Um, an old one would be [plays] 'You'll wonder where the yellow went when you brush your teeth with Pepsodent' for example.

Part 2

A: So presumably you have different kinds of music for different products, depending on what product you're advertising, do you?

B: Yes, for example, for a soft product (Like?) like shampoo or detergents in some cases, you would want some soft music, so it might sound a bit [plays].

A: So what's a hard product, then?

B: Well, cars, perhaps, er [plays] with drums and um for image, really, for a young image.

A: And talking of young, what about kiddies' products, like toys or …

B: Well, for younger children, they tend to be fairly jingly tunes that are used, a little bit mechanical sounding [plays] but then for more grown-up children or older children, perhaps there'll be something related to the pop charts, to pop music, or for Action Man, for example, that will be tough music: [plays] for example.

A: So for something like a breakfast cereal, for example?

B: It would tend to be jolly, or …

A: That's to wake you up is it in the morning?

B: To wake you up or healthy sounding, sort of American sounding [plays] Says both 'Good morning' and um 'Be healthy'. In this country we tend to joke a little bit more about it and perhaps [plays] 'Up you get!'

Part 3

A: So in your career, has there been any commercials that you particularly remember that either went very well or very badly or … Anything that sticks in your memory?

B: Yes, one for Tia Maria, which is a drink, um, when they gave me the words, or a list of words rather – sun, sand, sea – and said write something a little bit soully, please, like soul music, put the words in any order you like, and I really just about wrote the advert in the taxi on the way back to my house from the meeting.

A: Incredible. And what was it like?

B: Oh [plays] 'Tia Maria'. It did that and it then [plays] 'With the sound of the sand dum de dum … Get it together, with Tia Maria'. Excuse the voice.

Part 4

A: So how are you paid for this? Do you just get a flat fee?

B: I'm paid for doing a demonstration of how it might go, I will do what we call a demo. They listen to that and say 'Yes, let's finish it off.' I then do the final, for which I'm paid. I might also be paid for arranging it for a group of musicians. So I will use a synthesiser or a piano, to show them how it might be, and then we'll get an orchestra in or a set of musicians. Also when it goes on television I'm paid each time it's on, a little (That's nice) And each time it's put onto a new film, I'm paid some more too.

A: So it's not something you're thinking of giving up?

B: I don't think I can afford to give it up.

3C   The finished product

St Ivel Shape yoghurt has a light, fresh, fruity taste. A taste that comes shining through. Because St Ivel Shape yoghurt is virtually fat free. How refreshing. Say 'St Ivel' and you're in refreshingly good shape.

Unit 4   The island

4A   *The first half of the story*

EXERCISE 2

A boy lived in the woods, and his father told him never to go eastwards, but to play in the clearing by their hut, or to walk towards the west. For some years, the boy obeyed his father, but as he grew older, and the paths of the west became dusty with use, he felt himself drawn to the unknown trees and the green trackways, and one day he set off towards the east.

He found a lake and knelt down to drink, but the water was alive with savage fish, and he nearly lost a hand. He crouched by the shore and watched the fins swirl the water, and a stranger came up behind him so softly that the boy knew nothing until the man spoke.

'Let us see who can throw a spear the farthest.'

'Very well,' said the boy, and he won easily.

'Let us run around the lake,' said the man.

'I agree,' said the boy, and he won that too.

'Let me show you the island in the middle of the lake,' said the man.

'Do you like fish?' said the boy. 'I can see the island from here.'

The man whistled, and a boat came into sight, drawn by three flying swans. The man and the boy stepped into the boat, and were carried to the island.

But as soon as they landed, the boy wished that he had stayed at home, for the man knocked him down and left him, and went back across the lake. The boy felt his bruises – nothing was broken, although he ached from the fists. He limped about the island to find food, but there was little except berries and roots and – no shelter. He sat and watched the night come.

'If you would be good enough to dig an inch or so into the earth,' said a voice close by him, 'you would do me a great kindness.'

4B   *The second half of the story*

EXERCISE 2

Part 1

The boy was startled, for there was no one to be seen.

'I'm in the leaf-mould,' said the voice.

The boy scraped the last year's autumn, and underneath he found a skeleton lying yellow on the ground.

'I am much obliged,' said the skeleton. 'Now one more thing, if you will. Under that tree, just by the bole, there's a pouch buried. Would you bring it to me?'

The boy put his hand down by the bole, and found a tobacco pouch down in the soil, and a pipe, and flint.

'It would gratify me,' said the skeleton, 'if you would light the pipe and put it in my mouth.'

The boy did so, and held the pipe between the skeleton's teeth.

'Ah, thank you, thank you,' said the skeleton. 'It's the mice, you see. They nest in my ribs and only the smoke will move them. Such a torment they are, and such a blessing this is.'

The boy sat without moving until the skeleton had finished the pipe.

Part 2

'Now,' said the skeleton, 'you will want to know what you can do about the man who brought you here. Well, I'll help you. He's on his way now with dogs to hunt you for sport, so you must run up and down all over the island leaving tracks, and be sure to touch every tree. Then when he comes, hide at the top of a tree, and they will never find you.'

And that is what the boy did, and the dogs could not find him, for his scent was everywhere. At dawn, the man took them off, and went back to the land.

Part 3

'He will come at night,' said the skeleton, 'and it will be to drink your blood. But you must dig a hole in the sand, near where the boat is beached, and wait for him to start looking for you.'

All that day, the boy held the pipe for the skeleton.

'And remember,' said the skeleton. 'Don't return for a year. Then, if you will bring me a little tobacco, perhaps, it would be most beneficial, indeed it would.'

The boy hid in the sand until the man had disappeared among the trees, and then he ran to the boat and jumped in. As soon as they felt the movement, the swans flew back to the land, taking boat and boy with them safely among the deadly fish. And the boy went home, and stayed westwards for a year.

EXERCISE 4

At the end of the year, he made his way to the lake again. The swans were waiting. The island was unchanged.

'I've brought a new pipe and pouches of tobacco,' said the boy.

'You are more than considerate,' said the skeleton. 'The nesting season has been a great burden.'

The boy lit the pipe, and the mice were soon cleared.

'Can I do anything more to help you?' said the boy. 'You saved my life. Shall I bury you?'

'No,' said the skeleton. 'I would rather know the sun and the rain, the wind and the moon, and let them do their work. It's pleasanter here than in the dark.'

So the boy built a hut on the lake shore, and each day he came with the swans to light the skeleton's pipe, and to keep him company, until the sun and the rain, the wind and the moon had done their work, and nothing remained to tempt the busy mice.

Unit 5   Far from home

5B   *A foreigner in Germany*

EXERCISE 1

I do love being abroad, I like living abroad, I like feeling foreign, I like the novelty value of not really belonging here. You're constantly stimulated by the new culture and the new people, the language, just all these new impressions really stimulate the imagination and it's so inspiring. I find there's so much to write about, so much to write home and tell my friends about what I'm experiencing.

On the negative sides it's all … it's demanding, it can be too demanding and sometimes it's difficult to manage, and you often have to manage on your own. For example if you have a health problem and you have to try and explain your problem to a doctor who's not really following your pathetic attempt at the language or your English, and you're already ill, and you're trying to communicate exactly what's wrong, that can be problematic.

Trying to complain, often, trying to be assertive when in your own country you could easily firmly stand up for yourself, and I find in a foreign language that is difficult to convey, especially politely in the way that you would like. For example if you have something stolen, I remember having a coat stolen and I had to go to the lost property office and then try and describe it and I ended up drawing a picture, and this didn't seem to convey what I wanted to find.

Other things, negative things, you don't fully feel integrated in the society. You're always on the outside, and this can also be an advantage, you're looking onto a society, you're looking onto how other people are living, and as much as this is interesting, I think even if you can speak the language you don't fully get involved. And this can make you feel isolated and homesick, and then you begin to miss your own country. For example when people are sharing a joke, and even if you can follow the language, sometimes the humour is different (in fact usually the humour is different). And for example if you try to make a joke and it's not understood, there are a lot of cultural differences like that, when you can't really convey what you want to say. And you miss out on that banter between people, especially in public on public transport between strangers. You just can't possibly do that in another country without the freedom of speech, without being able to use the language like a native. And I find that frustrating, completely exasperating, because I feel I can't be myself.

5C Impressions of Malaysia

EXERCISE 1

I think I found some of the interesting things were just simple things like going shopping.

But at the same time felt quite nervous about that, because I didn't really know how to ask for these things.

It was easy to go to the supermarket at first, I think.

The people who were selling all this stuff were actually very pleased that you went there.

Yeah, but it's just the nervousness about the different system of what's there.

I think that's one of the big problems of being an expatriate.

I was viewed as something of an oddity because I travelled by bus.

A: I think I found some of the interesting things were just simple things like going shopping and finding food in sacks as opposed to food in packets like in the supermarket, going into small shops where there was sort of raw fish, and all sorts of different things hanging there, that you could just pick up – just a totally different way of shopping. But at the same time felt quite nervous about that, because I didn't really know how to ask for these things, but everybody else was asking for them, so you wanted to be part of it, but not really knowing how people bought in quantities and what they actually did with these things, so it was quite difficult. It was easy to go to the supermarket, but …

B: It was easy to go to the supermarket at first, I think, but in fact when one took the step and went to the 'Wet Market' as they called it, this huge building where all these as you say unpackaged things were, people, the people who were selling all this stuff were actually very pleased that you went there and not to the supermarket, and in fact you got a great deal of help and encouragement.

A: Yeah, but it's just the nervousness about the different system of what's there, and it's about trying to break into that, and you could actually just go there and never actually experience how people actually live on a daily basis.

B: I think that's one of the big problems of being an expatriate. I think probably most expatriates don't make that step, and they don't get into the way that the people who live in that country permanently exist. For example, public transport. I every day travelled by bus to the school I was working at, and this was considered to be dangerously odd, because I didn't have a car. Because all my colleagues had cars, and I was viewed as something of an oddity because I travelled by bus. I think probably most people didn't know how much the bus fares were or even what number of bus went to any particular place.

EXERCISE 3

A: I mean what I was amazed about was how people loved their food, you know, and took great pride. I mean they knew about all the fruit and how they would listen to it and shake it and (Bananas, remember?) … and pineapples and papayas. They knew when it was ready and when it wasn't, whereas to us here all apples look the same really – they're green or red – we don't know anything. They're much more in touch with nature and with what they eat, which is really, you know – with great respect for what they do eat and care about it …

B: Where we look for a 'sell-by' date, they would actually listen to a banana, and you would have the same result, really, yes.

A: I think generally people took great pride in everything that they did, in shops, selling things.

B: And also other sorts of skills which were available.

A: Well, tailoring was one of the things (Tailoring, yes), I suppose it was mostly the Chinese community that did that, but they took great pride in making garments, and making sure that everything was absolutely perfect fitting and (Yes). And also hairdressing was another thing that I found was really good, because you didn't just go in and sit there for a quick hair wash. They would massage your head completely for, you know, about ten minutes and really relax you.

B: And massage your ears.

A: Yeah, they sort of tickled your ears and things. But they just took great pride in … That was my experience that people did take great pride in what they did, which is quite different from here, where it's just a job. I mean I think it's a wonderful experience to live abroad, to witness these different things and to experience how other people do live, but I think it is quite hard to feel part of it, even although you make friends and are invited to share their lives a bit, it's I think it's quite hard to really be a part of it. You're always going to be different, and maybe that's OK.

Unit 6   The Louvre Pyramid

6A An architect's view

EXERCISE 2

I like the Louvre Pyramid because of its transparency, because you can just look through it, and it has a very light effect. It is not heavy and it is made of glass, and so it looks like a light object. And I like it for its contrast of shapes, because it is such a contrast to the Louvre building that in fact it doesn't interfere with the beauty of the Louvre, but it even, it emphasises the beauty of the Louvre. And in the evening when this pyramid is lighted, it's just a source of light to put the Louvre into a new light.

And this has for me also a symbolic meaning. And it is such an unexpected shape in this urban context, just to use a traditional shape of a pyramid built in new materials with new technologies, high-tech, and so on, that it is a completely surprising effect. So that people get shocked by it or they like it, but there is nobody who would be uninvolved or who could just pass and not notice this building. So it's something you have to look at. And I think this is also very important in building, and creating something in the cities, and exactly for example close to these historical buildings which are such a, they are so sensitive topics that nobody dares to touch them. I think the right thing is really to put something so contradictory to it that they stand in dialogue with each other and they don't even try to complement each other. Because it would have been the biggest mistake to try to build something similar to the Louvre, to put a building which would copy the Louvre, because it would just mean that we don't live in continuity, the architecture doesn't continue its history, but it would mean that architecture stands still on the level of the 17th century, and that would be a lie.

6B   Watch this space

EXERCISE 2

1   Well, what I have in mind, as you can see from the plans, is a very tall, thin and square-shaped building that rises right up some 300 feet. At the top it would have a circular space which could be used either for a restaurant or for special exhibitions, depending on what was required. I see this very much as being a mirror reflection, if you like, of the Eiffel Tower, so you'd have these two large, tall buildings, and certainly it would prove a new focal point for the city, one which I think people would go to for a variety of reasons, whether it's for the exhibitions, whether it's to eat there, or whether it's simply to enjoy the panoramic views that you would undoubtedly be able to enjoy from the top restaurant. And I do feel that if this could be achieved then we'd have a really major tourist attraction on our hands.

2   It is my idea to transform the area outside the Louvre into a park, with grass, trees, flower-beds, seats for people to sit on and a fountain in the centre, surrounded by a pond. There'll be sculptures from the Louvre building itself dotted about the park for people to admire outside the building as well as inside. In bad weather I suggest a retractable plexi-glass roof which could be put across so that the park would become an extension of the Louvre building itself. It would then attract more people, whatever the weather, and the style would marry very happily with the original building.

3   My idea for the square would be an adventure playground and funfair for children. This area would be bordered by trellis and would have lovely plants growing up, like passion flower, roses and clematis, and there would be a creche with childminders, where, obviously, the parents could leave their children and walk round the Louvre. The idea is, obviously, to get more families coming to this area. At the moment, you know, that's what we're lacking. In that area, there would be clowns and street entertainers who would be there. There's a seated area, where there would be a cafe, obviously, and the street entertainers would entertain while people were sitting there, while the parents were sitting there and the children were enjoying themselves on the various shoots and slides and swings that we have planned for the adventure playground area. I believe this would work. And some of the things that could be included would be things that were connected to the Louvre, such as face painting, or painting pictures generally, and making sculptures for the children. I think this would be a jolly good idea and would obviously attract more families to the Louvre and bring life to the square.

Unit 7   Technically speaking

7A   What's it about?

Part 1

1   What it actually is is that the pancreas, which is as far as I know a part of your body near the stomach which secretes a certain kind of hormone called insulin, stops working, and so you don't have the insulin. What insulin's used for is converting the sugar or the carbohydrate that you eat, converts it into energy.

2   So if you're a diabetic and don't know you're a diabetic the food that you're eating isn't being converted into energy, which is why you're so tired. And ultimately you need insulin to be able to live. So what a diabetic does is they inject insulin artificially, which should take the place of the insulin that the pancreas used to secrete.

Part 2

It's quite a heavy machine.

It's made of very sort of solid metal, quite shiny. You don't actually wash it, because you leave it after you've used it, which is very nice – it feels like it's sort of a something that people would use all the time.

Anyway, to use it you first of all have to make the dough.

And you very slowly mix the eggs with the flour until it becomes a sort of solid dough. And you have to knead this for quite a while until it becomes shiny and very flexible. You have to put it in the fridge for a while just to sort of cool it down and make it more manageable.

And then you cut it into small pieces, and put it into a sort of slot in the top of the machine, and turn the handle, and it comes out in sort of long flat sheets. You do this a few times.

If you want lasagne you can leave it as it is, or you can put it through again on another thing which has like little forked slots, which then cuts it into tagliatelle or spaghetti depending on what you want.

Part 3
Well the first one – the first person to go up of course wears a safety harness and is belayed from below.
If you're just right at the bottom of the cliff then the belayer doesn't need to tie herself onto anything, but if you're already higher up she'll have to secure herself to a boulder or a tree or whatever. So that if the first person does fall she's OK. She's not going to – well, the belayer herself won't be pulled off.

OK, so the first person starts climbing, and well she has to secure herself as she goes up, so she carries a certain number of little implements with her, things called rocks, friends, nuts and slings.

And a rock surface as you know is not smooth like a wall, there are certain features in the rock which enable you to protect yourself. And so as you go you might find a little crack and you put in a rock, which is a chock of metal of an uneven shape, so that you can slot it into the crack in such a way that it can't easily be pulled out again. So you slot that into the crack, put a carabiner through the sling attached to that, and then you clip your rope into it.

7B Kite racing

EXERCISE 2

1A: O.K., you're practising kite racing. What is it exactly?
B: Well, it's actually it's called a parakart, and it's a three-wheeler cart which is powered by a quadrafoil, which is a kite which look a little bit like a parachute. You've got four lines to it and you put it in the air and you go with the wind and that's – you get power by the kite with this little three wheeler going about 20, 25 miles an hour.
A: Can you ... Do you just go downwind, do you?
B: Well you actually go cross-wind, that's the same principle as land-yachting or sailing. Where you actually put the kite across the wind and you got a reach, and you go downwind and you also can tack which is going upwind. So you can do racing which is triangular.
A: How do you start off, what do you have to do? Can you show me?
B: Yes, you actually, what you actually do is you put the kite into the wind, the kite is full into the wind, you sit down on the cart, and you actually go sideways with the kite and then the actual power of the wind into the kite will give you this power this motion going into the wind.

2A: What about stopping? How do you stop?
B: Stopping is just a matter of ... there is no brake

on the cart, so you use the kite to use it as a brake or you turn very quickly on the sliding of the cart will actually make you stop, a little bit like skiing in a way, you know where you got a got a good turn and you will decrease your speed you see.
A: So you have to be careful not to fall over.
B: Well careful to fall over or make sure you anticipate that there may be a wall at the end and make sure you turn before the wall.
A: So today you're just practising. Could you show me how you do it?
B: Well, here we go! We've got the kite up. I'm sitting down on the cart now and I'm putting the cart on the side, and then you have to follow me quickly because I'm going very much faster than you do. And then you turn round and there you go.

Unit 8 GWR FM

8A On the air

EXERCISE 2

1 A call from a lady in Bristol, who has a roof full of bees, and she doesn't know what to do with them and it's scared all her children away, it's serious stuff, all her children have run away because the home is full of bees. She's looking for a bee-keeper. Do you wanna just pick up some bees? Seriously. Actually if you can help out it will be appreciated, just give me a call here at the radio station and we'll pass your number on to this lady. OK? If you wanna just pick up a whole swarmful of bees she's got 'em.

2 *More than just a house it's home, with Persimmon homes.* Persimmon homes, one of Britain's largest house-builders, are now completing new developments at Chipping Sodbury and Shepton Mallet. Surrounded by open fields and near the town centre, both developments are for larger than average two- to four-bedroom houses in great locations. Reserve any home from either development before June 6th and Persimmon will knock £1000 per bedroom off the asking price. This offer will end on June 20th, so for appointments to view call now on 0666 824721. *More than just a house it's home, with Persimmon homes.*

3 It's seven o'clock. The top story this hour. The 24-hour RNT rail strike starts at midnight. Chaos for Avon commuters. Inter City has already cancelled half a dozen trains tomorrow through Bristol and changed other services as well. People are being told to finish their train journeys tonight by 10 o'clock if at all possible. Inter City's admitting it can't get enough buses tomorrow to help.

Avon police are calling for clear guidelines after a

PC found himself in the dock for giving a teenager a clip round the ear. PC Steve Guscott was called after youths were tormenting an elderly couple in Minehead. One 15-year-old complained after he slapped him. The police officer's admitted assault at Bridgwater magistrates. He now faces the sack and losing his pension. Police federation spokesman Robin Hobbs says officers must be given better guidance. 'Society wants the police service to protect them. Unfortunately, um, in this type of situation, it doesn't tell police officers how to protect them. Society has to tell the police service exactly what it wants us to do to help them out.'
Meanwhile it's been revealed today that …

4 GWR FM weather for tonight. Fine clear cool night with a low of 8, then tomorrow dry and bright. A little bit cloudier and slightly cooler than today but still a high of 21. It should stay this way through Friday. By the way, today has been the warmest day so far this year with a high temperature of 23.

5 GWR FM Maria Carey at number 1 and *Any time you need a friend* on the Hot 7 at 7. Thanks for your votes for making the chart happen. Now we reward you with tonight's Record Recall. Get on those phones, tell us any three songs from tonight's Hot 7 at 7, and you just could win *In the Air Tonight*, it's a two-CD set, the greatest artists on Virgin Records including Phil Collins, Genesis, Meatloaf, Janet Jackson, Lenny Kravitz, UB40, Mr Peter Gabriel and more. Here's the numbers. Bristol 29, Bath 44 or Swindon 61 8888 for tonight's Record Recall. Good luck!

6M: All week we're looking for the daftest thing your Dad ever did … we want the daftest thing your Dad ever did. Good morning, Elaine.
E: Yes. When I was learning to drive, right, he was going to take me out in the car, and he said to me 'I'd better get the car off the drive, because the gears are so close together', so … he got in the driver's seat, he then, as soon as he put it in reverse, he went straight through the garage doors.
W: (laughter) Oh great.

7 All very smooth and easy on the motorways this morning. The trains of course are out of action today but the rush that we were expecting hasn't occurred. M4, M5 and M32 running pretty smoothly, M32 into town usual story though. City centre: busy on Bath Road through Brislington up to Three Lamps Junction and by the Broadwalk Shopping Centre in Knowle. Bumper to bumper around Templemeads and Old Market, but nothing out of the ordinary …

8: M: Here we go, Pete, three questions.
W: OK Pete. What football team have just been banned from the FA cup and fined?

P: Well Tottenham Hotspur. 600,000 wasn't it? A double whammy.
W: Ooh very good. You a bit of a Spurs fan then? (No, no.) In what film did Robin Williams play Peter Pan?
P: Er *Hook*.
W: Correct. And what's the Science Museum and Exhibition Centre by Templemeads called?
P: The Exploratory. (Oh yes)
W: Correct. Three of three. Well done.
M: And good morning Angela, again. (Good morning) Three for you. So, Pete got three, didn't he? (I know)
W: OK Angela, you've got to do it for the girls. What horse race meeting is on this week?
A: Ascot.
W: Correct. Which actor played Al Capone in *The Untouchables*?
A: Oh my God.
W: I'll give you a clue. Bananarama made a song about him.
M: Michael Caine. That was Madness.
W: Any idea?
A: No.
W: Oh, it was Robert de Niro. (Oh) Have a go at the last one. What's the museum down on the dock from Prince's Wharf called? (Oh God) Big museum there. (Oh)
M: Oh well you've lost it the women today.
W: OK. No, it's the Industrial Museum. (Oh yeah) Never mind, Angie.
M: Oh Angie, thanks for having a go. Tough luck, Hartcliffe. Well done, Pete.

9: Got Wimbledon starting next week. And Jeremy Bates, he did so well last week at the Stella Artois tournament, got to the quarter final. Guess what? At the Manchester Open he crashed out yesterday in the first round. So er never mind. But also at Wimbledon next week, they're going to ban players from spitting, which is about time, but I wish they'd stop all that grunting when they serve, you know that (grunts) or whatever they do, I hate it.

8B *A clip round the ear*

EXERCISE 1

Avon Police are calling for clear guidelines after a PC found himself in the dock for giving a teenager a clip round the ear. PC Steve Guscott was called after youths were tormenting an elderly couple in Minehead. One 15-year-old complained after he slapped him. The police officer's admitted assault at Bridgwater magistrates. He now faces the sack and losing his pension.

EXERCISE 2

1 The parents of the boy slapped by a police officer are angered by claims that he deserved it. Community Constable Stephen Guscott's been

swamped by offers to pay his £100 fine imposed for giving the 14-year-old boy a bloody nose. Solicitors St John Napier says the boy's parents are considering legal action. 'They feel that the publicity that has been generated by this case is extremely unfair and prejudicial. They are respectable business people who run their own business. They're deeply concerned by the press publicity, which they feel is unfair and wholly one-sided.'

2 The parents of the Minehead teenager clouted by an Avon and Somerset PC are considering legal action against some newspapers. PC Steve Guscott's been swamped by messages of support after being fined for giving the 14-year-old a bloody nose. He now faces the sack. St John Napier is representing the boy's family. He says they're angry at the way he's being portrayed in the media. 'Personally a lot of adjectives employed by the press in describing their son have been completely inaccurate and totally unpleasant – yob, hooligan, foul-mouthed 14-year-old. They have also, as a result of publicity, been subjected to obscene phone calls, threats, so on and so forth.'

EXERCISE 3

1 W: There's been loads of support this morning for local bobby Steve Guscott. And on our question of the day we're asking, 'Who gave you a clip round the ear, and for what?'
M: OK Jim's on the line.
J: Well when I was younger (Yeah) I was sitting on a little wall, and a policeman, it was a policeman, actually, the local bobby told me to get off the wall obviously for my own safety, it was quite tall the wall. I jumped off the wall, and he walked round the corner and I jumped back up onto it. He came back round the corner, told me to get down and he cuffed me. All right? (Yeah) You see? This is going back about 20 years ago when that was deemed as acceptable. I ran upstairs to me mum holding one ear saying 'This policeman cuffed me', so she politely cuffed the other ear saying that I must have done something wrong. (Laughter) So I come away with two cuffed ears, as they say.
M: Oh right. So where are you calling us from. Horfield Prison?
J: Er, no no no. Cos that was the turning point of my life. I never done it again, you see.
M: Yeah, never sat on a wall again.
W: There's a lesson to be learnt there.

2 C: Who gave me a clip round the ear? I had several clips round the ear at school.
M: Yeah. All of them deserved or not?
C: I would say so, yes. And invariably it was for messing about with water.
M: Ah. Balloons full of water (Yes). Crisp bags full of water (Yes). Serves you right. Did it do you any harm?
C: No it never. Certainly it did not.
M: That's the thing, isn't it. You know …

Unit 9 Loud and aggressive

9A From the 80s to the 90s

EXERCISE 2

I noticed around 91 was the first year I really noticed it myself, that music changed dramatically, with the upcome of Nirvana with their popular record *Nevermind* – it's very very loud music – maybe you can compare it with punk at the end of the 70s, where something just exploded. Here we have more political awareness again – you know, recession, and economics are very bad at the moment you know with the recession and everything, and ecology, and 50% of young people nowadays are from divorced homes, broken homes, and er it's sort of like a no-future generation at the moment trying to express its aggression, and this explodes in the music nowadays. Say for instance in the 80s popular music was like for instance Sting, Genesis, more poppy tunes, catchy tunes, light music where you didn't have to think too much. The 90s, they just jump on your face, actually. It's not so catchy, there's a message behind it, it grabs you.

9B Low Self Opinion

EXERCISE 1

I want to talk about the song by Henry Rollins, it's called *Low Self Opinion*, and in the song he speaks about a person who has no strong self opinion of himself, he projects hatred upon himself and upon others, and he builds up a wall around himself to try to keep people away instead of being a little bit more introspective and trying to find another side of his personality, and alienates himself basically from everyone else in the world, and has a generally difficult time in life. And he tries to offer advice a little bit to this person and like he's saying you know try some introspection, look at yourself a little bit, instead of always feeling so bad about yourself.

EXERCISE 2

I think you got a low self opinion man
I see you standing all by yourself
Unable to express the pain of your distress
You withdraw deeper inside
You alienate yourself
And everybody else
They wonder what's on your mind
They got so tired of you
And your self ridicule
They wrote you off and left you behind
You sleep alone at night
You never wonder why

All this bitterness wells up inside you
You always victimize
So you can criticize yourself
And all those around you

EXERCISE 4

What I like about the song is, well the music is very loud and I like loud music at the moment, because it's aggressive and it's a way to express yourself when you usually don't express your aggressions. You can maybe dance to it or scream or sing or whatever. And I also like – I feel like this person he's singing about actually, and it touches very deep in me and I feel like someone is talking directly to me and I like the ways he sings, it's very expressive, it's very loud and yeah it's generally my type of music. The music Henry Rollins makes, I have a feeling it's very personal anyway. He's a person actually from the streets, who's had a really pretty tough life. He's tattooed from head to toe, and he's a very aggressive person. When you see him on stage he's a very impressive person, but he's, also seems like a very dangerous person, very violent person. But again in his lyrics and in his music the other side comes out, where you feel that he's a person and he has a very soft side also. The band it seems more or less improvises on his lyrics. It's not as if the music was there first. It's like the lyrics were there first, it's like he's speaking about something, they make it into lyrics and the music is just like a soundtrack to it.

Unit 10   Sarajevo

10A   *Under siege*

EXERCISE 3

Part 1

I was not that frightened. Maybe I had a feeling that nothing was going to happen to me. And I had that very good cellar which belonged to the restaurant where I live, and not too many people down there, and a bit of food. And I have been living together with them for years, so they behaved in a lovely way. I spent nights and nights down in the cellar, and one of the persons who worked down there woke me up with a cup of coffee in the morning, and I was joking like being in a hotel. And I got food down there – but the most horrible thing was that you didn't know when to be in the cellar. I spent months, and first at the beginning I was really afraid to go up to my flat, which is on the second floor, but little by little you started to go up because you could have spent hours down, get out, and a shell fell. So, and we call it our kind of Russian roulette.

Part 2

It was dangerous going out, but it was dangerous staying in. For example, we had these alarms and we were told that we should go to the cellar. And I thought, you know, well I can't go downstairs 18

floors down, it's 314 steps. I've counted them. (So you stayed during the bombardment?) Yes, I stayed in a corner which I thought was safe. It was in a corner by the lift, and I just sat there and I really wasn't scared. (You weren't scared?) No, I wasn't scared. I thought you know if it's meant to kill me it'll kill me. What I was scared of really was of being wounded by a sniper. I was petrified. (This is when you're crossing from one building to another, is it?) Yes, because I mean we discovered that there was a sniper on the hill opposite, and he changed his place every day, so he got people on balconies, he got people even through a crack between two buildings and he shot at their legs, you know, crazy. And I really was petrified of being wounded or made an invalid.

Part 3

People had to live without any vitamins, without any fruit for months. And there were some, but so expensive, a kilo of potatoes, £40. I personally got only three potatoes in ten months, didn't know what to do with them. And onion, I got some onion from a friend, and I gave one to another friend. He couldn't believe it, he said, 'No, give me half of it, it's too much.'

And all the shops being just robbed, you could find something outside in the street, and especially books, because people were not interested very much in books. And a friend of mine showed me a beautiful history of art, and he opened it and he wrote in it 'I got it for seven cigarettes', and he said, 'I am going to keep it for ever.'

10B   *Survival*

EXERCISE 2

So we didn't have electricity, so we thought of all sorts of ways of cooking our meagre food. And luckily in my building, which is a high-rise building, we have a fire escape, which is made of metal, so people lit fires and cooked their food there. And some had grills, you know these portable things that you take when you go on a picnic, but I didn't have anything, so I found two bricks at a nearby building site, and found lots of things to burn, you know, all the combustibles from my small house, from my small flat, were burnt in order to make myself a pot of tea or a ... (You mean the furniture or ...?) Well even bits of furniture, you know, when you get shelled all the bits of furniture fall off. But unfortunately modern furniture is not made of solid wood, you know, but it's this chipboard whatever it's called, and you need something really combustible to start it going – once you do, it really burns well. So we looked everywhere, you know, for cardboard boxes, and in the loft I had saved my cardboard boxes from my computer and my printer, and it was really good imported cardboard. And when it got colder, I discovered that I could use these bricks for central heating. You know, I would put these bricks in between some cushions and they would give off the heat and keep a very small space warm. So hot tea kept me warm inside and the bricks warmed up the air around me.

10C Leaving Sarajevo

EXERCISE 1

And I remember on the road to Ljubljana sitting with a Bosnian friend. I caught sight of him – he was weeping, and discreetly wiping his eyes and trying to conceal it. Ten minutes later I was weeping. What made me weep? The sight of the calm, absolutely normal, familiar Croatian/ Slovenian countryside, with its haystacks and its fields and its trees and its little villages all untouched by war. I think for me it was an emotion for the lost Yugoslavia that got me then, although I couldn't in fact put it into words, but I had a little quiet cry to myself. And then I think that was the beginning of coming down to some kind of reality again. Although again Ljubljana with its prosperity was a shock, Ljubljana with its shops crowded with goods. I remember walking past a greengrocer's, and seeing all the fruit and thinking 'I haven't eaten any of that for five months.' I didn't want any, but the smell coming off the fruit was intoxicating.

Unit 11 Out West

11A Forefathers

EXERCISE 1

I once asked my grandfather about the family history, and he told me what he knew. And he said, well as far as he understood the first Roberts came over before the American revolution, that he came from Wales, was transported as a criminal to the penal colony of Georgia, and there he was an indentured servant for 10 years or so. And after he got his freedom, he decided to go west, and went to Alabama and then to Mississippi, and finally settled in Louisiana. And they were there for a number of years. And then when Texas still belonged to Mexico there was an offer of free land, and my great great grandfather, whose name was Silas Roberts, went there – because his wife had died, he had 18 children, and they got in a wagon and went to Texas to take advantage of the free land, to settle somewhere along the Brazos River. But no sooner had they set it up farming than Sam Huston and the Texas Army came and said, 'You're coming with us to fight in the battle of San Josento.' So he didn't have any choice, he left the 18 children, the eldest ones taking care of the youngest ones, and he went to fight in the Texas revolution. And he got his $40 in gold as a reward, came back, loaded all the children in a wagon, says you know 'We're not staying around here if they're going to fight,' and went back to Louisiana.

EXERCISE 2

Then the American Civil War, I had great uncles who fought in that. My great grandfather for some reason did not fight, but there were three great great uncles, I guess they would be, fought in the American Civil War. And my grandfather was very proud of the fact that they had served in the Confederate Army. One was killed at the Battle of Antietam and one was wounded at the Battle of Gettysburg and another was killed at another battle somewhere. And they're all buried in the Roberts cemetery, there's a big cemetery which has some graves in it that are 150 years old, you know it goes way out back. And he was particularly proud that one of these uncles had served in the Louisiana Tiger Regiment, that this was a very distinguished highly-decorated regiment. But I found out that this regiment in fact was a rather interesting one. When they were recruiting people for the Confederate Army they went into the prisons and told people they could come out of prison or stay there, and this was one of them. He apparently was a horse-thief and had been serving time in prison, and they asked him if he wanted to go and fight in the Confederate Army, and he said 'Sure!', so he did. And my grandfather said that he remembers this old man, that he used to sit on the front porch of the country store and chew tobacco, tell all these stories about the war, and that he and his brothers used to ask him sometimes, they'd say, 'How was the war?' He said, 'Oh, we had a great time.' He said, 'Well, did you ever shoot a Yankee?' He said, 'Yeah, dozens of 'em, just like shooting squirrels.' He had a rather interesting approach to war.

11B Great grandmother

EXERCISE 1

My great grandmother was a Cherokee Indian, and she had 16 children. And I met her when I was seven years old, she was 103 years old, and she was definitely an Indian, had long hair all the way down to her feet. My great grandmother was what they called a real pioneer woman. She was very tough. She didn't like to wear shoes because they hurt her feet, so she went barefoot most of her life.

EXERCISE 2

My grandmother told me the story once that my father and his twin brother were babies, and in those days they had to walk into town for a doctor, and it was quite a small town, they were about five miles away. There was this doctor who came once a month, sort of a circuit-riding doctor, and he was in town, so she took the babies in for a check-up. And it took a little longer than she expected, and so she was coming back carrying these two babies, and she was about a mile from the house, and she saw my great grandmother coming, barefoot as usual, with a big log over her shoulder. And she said to her, 'Mrs

Roberts, what are you doing out?' 'Well, I've come to get you, Bessie, because there's a wild bull loose in the forest.' So they started toward the house, and suddenly out of the woods came this bull. And my great grandmother just went over and broke this log over this bull's head. And the bull went back in the forest. That was the way it was, she was that kind of woman.

EXERCISE 3

She was a young girl at the time of the American Civil War, maybe 14 years old, but married to my great grandfather at 14. And he was away, and at the end of the war there were a lot of these bandits coming through robbing farms. And she was by herself, and this band came up and started to steal the meat out of the smoke-house. And she grabbed a rifle and started shooting at them. And they went to the next farm – they didn't stick around. So it was one of the few farms that wasn't robbed by the bandits.

Unit 12   Jigsaw of a village

12A   The pieces of the jigsaw

EXERCISE 2

GROUP A

Part 1

A: What kind of people do you get coming in here? Is it mostly local?
B: It's a cross-section. Well, we get passing trade. We do accommodation, so we get a lot of foreign visitors, like, you know.
C: Americans, Australians (Kiwis), people from the continent, now …
B: Japanese, Chinese.
A: Is that people passing through, or tourists coming to this area?
B: Tourists coming to this area, also people passing through. I'm ex-navy, so we get a few naval personnel in here (Squawk!).
A: That's the parrot, is it?
C: That's the parrot. That's Alex.

Part 2

A: Yes, sir.
B: Yeah, the sausages. What are the different kinds you have?
A: We have home-made pork, home-made pork with herbs, or home-made chipolatas.
B: What are these big ones here?
A: Those are jumbos. They're the same sort as home-made pork.
B: You make them, do you? I think I'll try the jumbos, actually. Maybe half a pound, eh?
A: The jumbos?
B: How much are they?
A: £1.34 per pound … There you are, sir. 85.
B: OK Thanks very much.
A: Thank you.

Part 3

A: The majority are four-year-olds, then I've got five- and six-year-olds as well.
B: And how many in the school altogether?
A: Just over 100.
B: Oh, it's quite a small school.
A: Yes, but the numbers are going up quite rapidly, so we'll be squashed into the classrooms.
B: What's it like teaching children of different ages in the same class? Is that a problem?
A: Um no it's not a problem. It's very taxing. You have to be very organised, because you have to set different levels of work for all the different children. So you can't just set one thing for them.
B: Do the bigger children help the smaller children?
A: Yes, that's the nice thing about it, yes, that you can, you can pair them off with a more able child and a less able. Yes, that's rather nice.

Part 4

A: And I'll have the wine list … Um … Yes, the Cornish fish soup for me, and the suprème of duck (Yes). And we'll have a bottle of Sancerre, number 28.
B: Yes, I'm having the same, the leek and almond, and the (And the turbot?). Yeah.
C: And a bottle of Sancerre? (Yeah) OK.
B: Thanks … They've got French waiters as well.

Part 5

Maybe they tried, maybe some of them were humble enough and faithful enough to continue to worship Him, to continue to keep those commandments, but as they came into all the comparative luxury of the Holy Land – out of the wanderings in the wilderness, to all those wonderful fruits, all that flowing water and abundant crops, it was very tempting for them to adopt their own gods, and they turned away from the one true God.

GROUP B

Part 1

A: Hello Chris!
B: Hello, George. How are you doing?
A: Morning.
C: Hello.
A: What would you like then, sir?
B: Um, a pint of 6X please. What about you Adrian?
C: Um … I'll have a half. (Just a half?)
B: Right, that's one and a half of 6X. (Taking it easy are you? A half this week is it?) Have you got any crisps?
A: Yes, yes we have. We have plain or cheese and onion.
B: I'll have some plain actually please – that'll be fine.
A: Yes, right then, here you are sir.

Part 2

A: I started my job here last September, so I've been here about seven months. So at this stage my wife and I are finding our way around the community.

B: What do you do apart from your work in the church?

A: Well, the whole of my life is being a pastor to the community. Therefore I'm available for people to talk to confidentially about any problems they've got. If they want to get married or they have a bereavement in the family, or they've got a baby they want to baptise. These are the normal things of course that vicars get up to. But I don't just work one day a week.

Part 3

Then you put the number in there. That's right. Right, where did we get to? 'Bride'. Can you find 'bride'? Begins with? 'b'. Then the next letter is 'r'. You want 'r', don't you? 'br'. 'Bride' ... Hijah! ... Here you are then. I've got a nice sheet for you. 'P' (This is extra hard for me, it is.) OK. 'P' sheet. If you can go over the 'p's with your pencil, then do some 'p's of your own, and then down the bottom here you've got to count up how many 'p's there are. They're all hiding. See if you can find them all – all right, good boy – and then count them up, put a ring round them, and then count them up and put the number in that box there. Right? Put your name on it first at the top. Would you like to give them out? Thank you. (I've already got one.) Did we find 'bride'?

Part 4

A: What are you doing at the moment in the class?

B: We're doing some projects on Europe. We have to choose one of the countries that belong to the EC. We do English, Maths. We've just had these three people in who've been, for a couple of days, who've been teaching us Science.

A: Can you tell me about the project? What country did you choose?

B: Oh, I'm doing Austria. You've got to ... We've got a sheet and there's these things listed and we've got to put them down in a book 'cause we're making a book. You've just got to say about Austria really.

A: What about you? What country are you doing?

C: I'm doing France 'cause I thought it might be interesting. But not many people have got anything about France.

A: Have you found out anything about it yet?

C: Yeah. I've found out, like, what animals they've got. And I've made this forest thing. It's quite good, actually.

Part 5

A: Our meat, most of it is local, we get it from Malmesbury. The bacon comes from Bromham. That's made the old-fashioned way of salting it and drying it out, so it gives it a much stronger flavour. It's not like this soppy bacon that you get in packets, it's proper bacon. And the cheese we do, that comes from Cheddar, that's a little farm,

they still make their own cheese.

B: Still made in the traditional way?

A: Yes, with the cheesecloth and everything on it, yes, and the rind. And we cook hams the old-fashioned way.

B: And do you make your own things, like do you make pies and things?

A: Yeah – no, we don't make pies. We do sausage, and I make, you know, different things for barbecues. But sausages, basically sausage and faggots I make. And that's about – that's, you know, what a traditional butcher would have made years ago.

12B   Living in Box

EXERCISE 1

Part 1

There's no place like Box. It has its own special feelings, you know, the community here is really good, you know the community spirit. We have you know with all these shows and that, the village comes together. It's very very good.

Part 2

A: We moved down from London 10 years ago. We lived in Central London, in Islington, and we've never lived outside London before, but because we had two young children we decided that it may be better for them if they was brought up in the country.

B: And do you like it here? Are you glad you came?

C: Oh yeah, we've had a good time down here, haven't we?

B: What's it like as a village? Is it a nice village to live in?

A: (Oh yeah, yeah) Very nice village to live in. People are friendly, and we've got a very very good groundsman who keeps the village really neat and tidy and very attractive in the summer. We've got a very nice local school, it's got its own little swimming pool.

Part 3

I think it's a very fine community. I mean the first thing that struck me was the number of community groups catering for practically every interest, both athletic and academic, well-supported and working to a very high standard. And supporting one another, too. If there's a fund-raising event on, then people will rally round and support that event; it doesn't matter whether you are giving money to repair the church spire or helping the badminton club to provide some new facilities.

Part 4

A: I think as long as you speak the language properly and you can understand people you can blend quite well into the village life. And I think in England the village life is very important. You know, you have people playing cricket in the afternoon, you have the church, you have the school, you have the little shops, and you've got a really good social life, which is more difficult to have in bigger towns.

B: Is English village life very different from French village life, do you think?

A: I think it is. I think the English people in general are more sociable. They tend to invite people which they don't necessarily know much more easily in their home. And there is the famous pub, which you go round and have pint, you know, and you meet people. So I think they're generally more sociable than maybe the French would be.

Part 5

A: It's good because we've got a school near, and there's some clubs down in the halls and that, so it's quite amusing.

B: What about the school? What do you think of the school? Is it good?

A: Yeah, well we've just recently got a new headmaster, and he's made some changes.

B: What's he done?

A: Um, he's made new rules and stuff, and bought loads of new books. He's really touched it up, really.

Unit 13   All you need is love?

13A   *A partner for life*

EXERCISE 2

A: What do you think it is that attracts people to each other, that makes people want to be together?

B: I think that perhaps unfortunately in the initial stages it's the physical appearance that attracts. I think unless you find somebody attractive, unless there's something about them – it could only perhaps be the way they smile or they laugh, or a twinkle in their eye, or the way a curl falls over their forehead. But something like that has to make you interested enough to find out more about that person, unless that's there I think you just don't bother. So initially physical attraction I think is all-important.

A: Why do you say 'unfortunately'?

B: Because in fact it shouldn't be what somebody looks like that is important. You should be able to look beyond the physical appearance and see what sort of a person he or she is, whether they're selfish or selfless, whether they're kind, caring. But I think initially you're not bothered with that. That comes perhaps later.

A: In pop songs and magazines and newspapers and so on, the idea of falling in love is always emphasised, so people have this idea that you have to fall in love. Do you think this is misleading for people? Do you think people expect something that in fact doesn't exist?

B: Yes I do, in fact I think we can probably lay the blame for the high percentage of divorces – it's a third I think now isn't it? I think one in three people get divorced. Probably as far as I can see it, the reason is that they go into marriage or a relationship with a very romantic view of love which I think has been created by the pop songs, by all the love stories, by the Barbara Cartland novels, etcetera, that young people read. Really, you meet someone, you fall in love, and that's it, it's the beginning, they live happily ever after. And I think that's the problem, because people just expect that, and it's not like that.

A: So what is it, do you think, that really sustains a relationship, that keeps a relationship going?

B: Well, I think you have to differentiate between falling in love with somebody, which I see as more superficial, and loving somebody, which I see as a deeper emotion and one that perhaps lasts. Falling in love is superficial attraction, being attracted to somebody physically, having fun together, whereas loving somebody I think is an emotion that grows, it comes with shared experiences, perhaps enjoying doing the same things together, shared hobbies, shared interests. Suffering together as well, going through the bad times, helping each other, supporting each other. I think all that needs time to grow, and I'd call that love, and I think that's what makes a relationship last.

13B   *An arranged marriage*

EXERCISE 2

C: We were neighbours, our parents knew each other very well, we went to the same schools, taught by the same teachers, played in the garden and around, and it was only later on, many years later on, when our parents thought it was a good idea to bring us together. But we weren't dragged into marriage, we had the option to say no, from my point of view there was no objection. I think Gurmit had a slightly different view, but as far as I'm concerned it's worked out very well. People perhaps have got a distorted view of arranged marriages. No partner is dragged into a marriage, we have complete freedom to say no or yes. Equally if some, if children come up with the option, then the parents have equal option to say yes or no whether they like it.

A: With your marriage, the idea though came from the parents?

C: The idea came from Gurmit's mother. That's how, she approached my mother, and both of them decided yes perhaps it is. We are of similar age, have slightly different hobbies and outlooks, but it's worked very well.

A: And what would be the, in an arranged marriage like this, what would be the important thing in deciding on a suitable partner for you, would it be social background or age or …?

C: Certainly, because one of the main things first, before any couple is introduced to each other, the parents will do a fair amount of research about the, if it's the bride's family they will certainly do a research on the bridegroom's family side, what's the family like in terms of general behaviour, their wealth, what's their standing in the society, what's the bridegroom education like, is he working or not, how well is he off, really. Because at the end of the day any parent is interested in seeing that their daughter does settle down in a well-established family.

EXERCISE 4

A: In your case in fact you knew each other as children (We knew each other as children). But in other cases where the couple doesn't know each other, isn't there a danger that they, they get married – they don't have much chance to get to know each other before marriage? Is that right or …?

C: Yes, that is quite possible, yeah.

A: So isn't there a danger that they then discover that in fact they don't like each other very much?

C: Now you have to, it's like going on a course, isn't it? On an educational course, you may not like it but attending the class and learning to live with it, learning to acquire the knowledge and then use it to your benefit, you have to give and take.

A: Well, I think what very often happens now in England, say, is that a couple meet, and they get to know each other (Yeah), and then maybe at a later stage they introduce their partner to the parents. And I think a very common attitude is that, well it's not the parents who are getting married, it's the children who are getting married so they should decide. What do you think about that?

C: Um, I think parents have had, parents generally have perhaps a better experience than the children. I think they probably don't give them the same amount of credit perhaps that is due. As I said, no parent wants to see their children's marriage sort of break up, so certainly in our society, in the Asian society, they will go to great lengths to make sure that the couples are suitable, even before they're introduced. If you look at from the bridegroom's side, once he has a job and he's settled, might have his own house or he's nearly ready to own his own house, the parents would be encouraging him to get married. Obviously if he knows someone then the situation is a little easier. If not, then they would sort of pass the word within the family group that they are looking for a bride, you see. So that's how the system works. And an introduction is then sort of arranged, and at any stage if the situation doesn't look right it can be called off. It can be called off by parents or by the couple involved.

A: I think for a lot of young people in the West, the main idea that they'd have in their minds would be falling in love and being in love (Yes). And you'd fall in love with somebody and then this would be your partner. What do you think of this? Is this very superficial, do you think?

C: I think it is very superficial. I think that love comes out of a relationship really. Your initial thoughts may be you like somebody because they look right, they probably dress right, they are to the right level of education, may have the right sort of financial background, there could be many aspects which starts a relationship. And it obviously depends how the couple work at that relationship to make that relationship work. And the fondness for each other comes out of that, and the tolerance to give and take comes out of that relationship.

Unit 14   Get it?

14A   Children's jokes

EXERCISE 1

1 What time is it when an elephant sits on your fence?
Time to get a new one.
2 Have you read 'Thirty Years in the Saddle' by Major Bumsore (= *made your bum sore*)?
3 Knock knock (Who's there?) Lena (Lena who?) Lena (= *Lean a*) little closer and I'll give you a kiss.
4 Why did the owl 'owl (= *howl*)?
Because the woodpecker woodpecker (= *would peck 'er*).
5 Why did the chicken cross the road? (I don't know.) To get to the other side.
6 *Girl:*   I wish we lived in the olden days.
Teacher: Why?
Girl: Because then we wouldn't have so much history to learn.

EXERCISE 2

1 Why was six afraid of seven?
Because seven eight (= *ate*) nine.
2 Knock knock (Who's there?)
Boo (Boo who (= *hoo*)?)
No need to cry – it's only a joke.
3 Why did the chewing gum cross the road?
It was stuck to the chicken's leg.
4 Why did the duck cross the road? (I don't know.) It was the chicken's day off.
5 Why did the dinosaur cross the road? (I don't know.) Because chickens weren't invented yet.
6 Why did the fly fly?
Because the spider spider (= *spied 'er*).
7 When were there only three vowels? (I don't know.) Before you and I (= *U and I*) were born.
8 What did the policeman say to his tummy?
You're under a vest (= *arrest*).
9 Knock knock (Who's there?)

Isabel (Isabel who?)
Isabel (= *Is a bell*) necessary on a bicycle?
10 'How to Save Money' by Iona (= *I own a*) Fortune.
11 What do you call a reindeer with no eyes?
(I don't know – what do you call a reindeer with no eyes?)
No idea (= *No-eye deer*).

EXERCISE 3

1 This young lad went to a farm for an interview 'cause he wanted a job. And he had crutches. The farmer said to him 'Are you strong?' He said 'Yes.' He said 'Have you ever had any accidents?' He said 'No.' And the farmer said, 'Well why are you on crutches, then?' And he said 'Oh, that wasn't an accident. The bull did it on purpose.'

2 Once there was a man and he went into a shop and bought a horse. And he got on the horse and said 'Giddy up', but the horse didn't move. So he tried again and again but it still wouldn't move. So he asked the shopkeeper how you get the horse to go, and the shopkeeper says 'You have to say "Thank goodness".' And the man asked the shopkeeper how you made it stop, and the shopkeeper said 'You have to say "Help".' And so the man got on the horse again and said 'Thank goodness' and the horse went galloping off. And they were coming to a very big cliff, and the man had forgotten the word to stop, and he was trying to think, and when they were almost at the edge, he shouted 'Help!' and the horse suddenly stopped just when they were about to go off the edge. Then he said 'Thank goodness!'

3 Well this American guy was going round the sights of London, and he goes 'Hey cab, get here, I want to have a look round London.' And he goes 'OK get in.' So they go past Big Ben, he goes 'What's that?' and the cab driver goes 'That's Big Ben', and he goes 'How long did that take to build?' 'That took 100 years' and he goes 'My lot could build that in a week.' So they go down a bit further and they see Buckingham Palace and he goes 'What's that?' and the cab driver goes 'That's Buckingham Palace' and he goes 'How long did that take to build?' '900 years.' 'Oh that was long,' and he goes 'My lot could build that in a fortnight.' And he walks on a little bit further they go over London Bridge, and he goes 'What are we on?' and he goes 'Don't know. It wasn't there this morning.'

14B The Bricklayer

EXERCISE 1

A striking lesson in keeping the upper lip stiff. Now wait, wait … is given in a recent number of the Weekly Bulletin of the Federation of Civil Engineering Contractors, which prints the following letter from a bricklayer in Golders Green to the firm for whom he worked:

EXERCISE 2

See page 48.

EXERCISE 3

I then continued to the top, banging my head against the beam and getting my fingers jammed in the pulley. When the barrel hit the ground, it bursted its bottom, allowing all the bricks to spill out. I was now heavier than the barrel, and so started down again at high speed. Halfway down I met the barrel coming up, and received severe injury to my shins. When I hit the ground, I landed on the bricks, getting several painful cuts from the sharp edges. At this point I must have lost my presence of mind, because I let go of the line. The barrel … The barrel … The barrel then came down, giving me another heavy blow on the head, and putting me in hospital. I respectfully request sick leave.'

Unit 15   In black and white (1)

15B   The lecture (Part 1)

EXERCISE 1

What we see here is a 16th century German engraving. Engraving is one of the oldest print-making techniques, discovered by goldsmiths who used it to make designs on jewellery. For it, you use a sharp tool called a graver, and a copper plate which is the basis on which the picture is made. You push the graver into the copper and this makes then a line by cutting away the copper and you lift up your graver at the end which gives the line a sharp point. Your possibilities are limited because of the way the technique is. You can see on this as well that you can make little cross-hatches as you see on the clothes of the people and in the tree, you can make little dots – you can see that on the grass – but it's not an easy line, it's quite a sharp, clear-cut line, and that is typical of the engraving, but most typical thing is that sharp point and sharp clearness of the line.

This here is another technique, called an etching. The plate is covered with a layer of wax, and this is then blackened with a candle so that you have a dark plate, you use a sharp tool, a needle, an etching needle, and with it you make a drawing in the wax. You then put your plate in the acid, and the acid will bite the line in the plate. Then you print it, which you do in the same way as an engraving: you clean off all your wax first and then you rub black ink over the whole plate and then you wipe it off again with a piece of cloth or with your hand. This makes the whole plate nice and clean except for the lines where the ink will stay because the lines have been bitten in it. You then take a piece of damp etching paper, put that on the plate, the whole thing goes through an etching press, and the ink will be sucked out of these deep lines and lay on the paper.

15C The lecture (Part 2)

EXERCISE 1

This is a woodcut by the Dutch artist Herman Gordijn, and it's called *Lida at the Table*, and made in 1984. For a woodcut, we use a piece of plank wood, which is the tree cut in the length. You use a tool called a gouge. The interesting thing with a woodcut is that it's in a way the reverse of the previous two techniques. Here what we're going to print is that what is left over and everything we want to be blank is cut away. The tool is pushed in the wood, along with the grain, and again it's quite restricting and controlled, and you need quite a bit of strength for it. By leaving an area completely untouched, you'll get the black part, as we can see here on the back of the chair and on the skirt from Lida, as well on the table, while that space under the table and on top of the table and on the wall is completely cut away. So where it's white, it's more work than where it's black. The effect of the woodcut is very sharp and clear in its final conclusion. There is a very sharp division between black and white. Also if you look at the woodcut, you will notice the grain of the wood still present in the line and again that is one of the charms of the woodcut.

EXERCISE 3

This is a mezzotint from around 1720–30. It's made on a copper plate, you need copper which is really good and hard. And you have a tool called a rocker. A rocker has lots of tiny little points. This tool you rock over the plate, and it goes over the plate in all directions, up down, up down, you go sideways, you go many many times over your whole copper plate till the whole plate is fully covered by tiny little indentations. If you would print that it would be completely black. Tiny little bits of copper are standing on the side, and this is called the burr, and this burr then is either put back into the little hole or is scraped away. And that's the way how you can make a lot of different grades and shades in black from the very dark velvety black to the light. So again like in the woodcut the more work you've done, the lighter it is. You work from dark to light. This work by the Irish mezzotinter James McArdell is particularly beautiful. He was one of the best mezzotinters ever, and you see the lovely soft effect on the dress, in her face, and on the woman's bonnet.

Unit 16   In black and white (2)

16A   Frame Story II

EXERCISE 4

In the foreground of the picture there is a house, looks like a deserted house. The curtains are blown by the wind, it's open, and there is a verandah looking out on the sea. The house looks abandoned but still there is a cat, which makes me think well there must be some people still living in the house. But the way the curtains are blown looks as if there was nobody to care for it. And the birds sitting on the window, they just suggest that there is nobody to be afraid of, they can come and take over and build a nest, probably. There is a letter in the letter box, unopened, and probably somebody left it there and it hasn't been found. Although it's in an obvious place, nobody took it out to read. The house is, well this whole view is very ambiguous. The house suggests on one hand cosiness and home and a romantic life, just sitting there on a rock looking over the sea, a very unique view of the sea and the mountains. And on the other hand it has something abandoned.

In the background of the picture there is a couple. They are lovers, and they're emerging out of the sea. The man is holding the woman in his arms, and looks sad, and he looks as if he was comforting her. And they are just miles and miles away from this house, so it looks like a contrast – people without a house and a house without people. And they both need each other, these people need a home and this house and the cat, they want their people. And they just seem to be very far away from each other. And there seems to be a stream between the sea and the house, as if the sea was flowing into the house, into the verandah.

I like the picture very much. It's, I think it's very powerful, and it gives me lots of associations.

16B   The artist's version

EXERCISE 2

This is one of my own mezzotints. When I was a student with a scholarship in Poland I learned how to do this, because it's not often that you have a chance of learning it nowadays. The picture you see here is called *Frame Story*. It's a story about a story about a story, and I made it quite a while ago. On it you see my house in Amsterdam, the front door, number 24 is in the room, and a letter comes through the letter box. In my room you see my cat laying there, she's deep asleep, on the window little wooden birds are sitting that I bought in Poland, and the curtain waves wild. Behind the wall we see Scotland and this is one of the fascinating things an artist can do. There is no limit to place, time, everything can be mixed together, the artist is a free person. On it we see the island of Raasay on the West coast of Scotland, the little path that I often walked on when I was in Scotland comes here into my room. It is a nostalgic image, in which we see the sea, and a couple emerging out of the sea vaguely into the sky, and I leave it to you to guess from who the letter is.

16D Extension: the making of Frame Story II

EXERCISE 2

To make a mezzotint is a very long and laborious job, and it's probably for this reason it's not very popular. A plate like this, which is about 30 by 40 centimetres, took me two weeks to rock, and that means simply to make it black, you haven't started working on it yet. And when I say two weeks I literally mean four hours a day. You couldn't do more because your arm is really quite sore by then. To make the image out of this complete black plate took me another six weeks – just to do the sky was about two weeks of scraping, because to take the burr off the plate again is a long and very slow technique. The lighter it is, the longer it takes, and that's why it's not very popular any more nowadays. Things like the birds are not touched; they are the original black. And in the curtain you can see how the dark and the light slowly interplay just like a painting, the reason why it was invented. I made mezzotints for a long time, about 15 years, but then I felt that this very restricting way of working was too much and I stopped making them now, and I paint now in oils.

Unit 17 *The Great Ruby Robbery* (1)

17A *The opening scene*

EXERCISE 1

(R = Remanet; O = O'Byrne; H = Harrison;
M = Maclure; B = Bertha; G = Gregory;
N = News vendor; P = Postman;
C = Constable; I = Inspector)

Scene 1: Outside Lady Maclure's house
R: Well, thank you for a lovely evening. Goodnight, Nora.
H: Goodnight.
R: Goodnight, Sir Justin.
O: I'll see you to the door … You looked charming tonight, Miss Remanet. Those rubies are magnificent on you.
R: You think so? Well, I'm glad you do. But it's goodbye tonight, Sir Justin, for I go next week to Paris.
O: No! you don't mean that? Oh, Miss Remanet, I'm so sorry … And yet, after all, perhaps …
R: Yet, after all, what?
O: Yet, after all – nothing.
R: That might do for an Englishman, but it won't do for me. You must tell me what you mean by it.
O: Miss Remanet. Miss Remanet – Persis – shall I tell you the reason why? Because I like you so much. I almost think I love you!

R: And yet you're not altogether sorry that I'm going to Paris!
O: No, not altogether sorry, and I'll tell you why, too, Miss Remanet. I like you very much, and I think you like me. For a week or two, I've been saying to myself, 'I really believe I must ask her to marry me.' The temptation's been so strong I could hardly resist it.
R: And why do you want to resist it?
O: These … rubies are why. Persis, you're so rich! I'd never dare to ask you.
R: Sir Justin, it's most unkind of you to say so; either you oughtn't to have told me at all, or else – if you did –
O: Oh, don't say that! I couldn't bear to offend you. But I couldn't bear, either, to let you go away – well – without having ever told you. Persis, I've cared a great deal for you – a great great deal – and had hard work many times to prevent myself from asking you. And I'll tell you the plain reason why I haven't asked you. I'm a man about town, not much good, I'm afraid, for anybody or anything; and everybody says I'm on the look-out for an heiress – which happens not to be true; and if I married you, everybody'd say 'Ah, there! I told you so!' Now, I wouldn't mind that for myself; I could snap my fingers at them; but I'd mind it for you, Persis. I couldn't bear to think people should say, 'There's that pretty American girl, Persis Remanet, who's thrown herself away upon that good-for-nothing Justin O'Byrne, a regular fortune-hunter, who's married her for her money.' So for your sake, Persis, I'd rather not ask you; I'd rather leave you for some better man to marry.
R: But I wouldn't! Oh, Sir Justin, you must believe me. You must remember –
H: Why, Justin, what's keeping you? The horses'll catch their deaths of cold; and they were clipped this morning. Come back at once, my dear boy!
O: All right, Nora, I won't be a minute. We can't get them to answer this precious bell. I don't believe it's working! But I'll try again, anyhow! … Is that your room with the light burning, Miss Remanet? The one with the balcony, I mean? Quite Venetian, isn't it? Reminds one of Romeo and Juliet. But most convenient for a burglary, too! Such nice low rails! Mind you take good care of the Remanet rubies!
R: I don't want to take care of them, if they make you feel as you say, Sir Justin. I don't mind if they go. Let the burglar take them! … Goodnight.
O: Goodnight.

17B *The plot thickens*

Scene 2: Miss Remanet's bedroom
R: Come on! Come on! … Come in!
B: Good morning, Miss.

R: Bertha. Send for the police at once, and tell Sir Everard that my jewels are stolen!

B: Yes, Miss.

R: 'Yes Miss'? Is that the best she can do? My rubies are gone, and she says 'Yes Miss'? … Come in.

M: Why, my dear – reading? Then you've found them again, I suppose. Bertha told us you'd lost your lovely rubies!

R: So I have, dear Lady Maclure. They're gone. They've been stolen. I forgot to lock my door when I came home last night, and the window was open. Somebody must have come in, this way or that, and taken them.

M: Are you quite sure you put them in the case, dear?

R: Quite confident, Lady Maclure. I always put them there the moment I take them off; and when I came to look for them this morning, the case was empty … Lady Maclure, do you consider that maid of yours an honest woman?

M: Yes, I should think so, on the whole. Yes.

R: I'm glad you think that's so; for I can't make her out at all. She's too quiet for my taste, somehow; so silent, you know, and inscrutable.

M: Oh my dear, don't blame her for silence; that's just what I like about her. It's exactly what I chose her for. Such a nice, noiseless girl; moves about the room like a cat on tiptoe; knows her proper place, and never dreams of speaking unless she's spoken to.

R: Well, you may like them that way in Europe, but in America, we prefer them a little bit human.

Scene 3: Miss Remanet's bedroom

B: The gentleman from the police, my lady. Mr Gregory.

G: Lady Maclure, Miss Remanet. Now then. The first thing we have to do, is to satisfy ourselves whether or not there has really, at all, been a robbery. We must look through the room well, and see you haven't left the rubies lying about loose somewhere. Such things often happen. We're constantly called in to investigate a case, when it's only a matter of someone's carelessness.

R: I'm quite sure I took them off and put them back in the jewel case. Of that I'm entirely confident. There isn't a doubt possible.

G: I should say that settles the matter. Our experience is that whenever people are perfectly certain, beyond the possibility of doubt, they put a thing away safely, it's absolutely sure to turn up where they say they didn't put it. So if you don't mind, I'll just have a little look around … Well, they don't seem to be here, do they …

R: As I told you.

G: … So now, if you please, we'll proceed to investigate the servants' boxes.

M: Bertha, go downstairs, and see that none of the other servants come up, meanwhile, to their bedrooms.

G: No, no. This young woman had better stop here with Miss Remanet – strictly under her eye – till I've searched the boxes. For if I find nothing there, it may perhaps be my disagreeable duty, by and by, to call in a female detective to search her.

M: Why, this is my own maid, Mr Gregory, and I've every confidence in her.

G: Very sorry for that, my lady, but our experience teaches us that if there's a person in the case whom nobody ever dreams of suspecting, that person's the one who has committed the robbery.

M: Why, you'll be suspecting myself next!

G: Your ladyship's just the last person in the world I should think of suspecting.

Scene 4: Miss Remanet's room

G: Now then, you're sure you were wearing the rubies when you got back to Hampstead last night?

R: Quite sure. I came back in Mrs Harrison's carriage, and Sir Justin O'Byrne, who accompanied us, noticed them and advised me to take care of them.

G: Oh, Sir Justin O'Byrne! He came back with you in the carriage, then? And did he sit on the same side with you?

M: Really, sir, if you're going to suspect gentlemen in Sir Justin's position, we shall none of us be safe from you.

G: The law, my lady, is no respecter of persons.

M: But it ought to be of characters. What's the good of having a blameless character, I should like to know, if – if –

G: If it doesn't allow you to commit a robbery and get away with it? Well, well, that's true. That's perfectly true – but Sir Justin's character, you see, can hardly be called blameless.

R: He's a gentleman, and he's quite incapable of such a mean and despicable crime as you dare to suspect him of.

G: Oh, I see! Sir Justin's a friend of yours! Did he come into the porch with you?

R: He did, and if you have the insolence to bring a charge against him –

G: Calm yourself, madam. I do nothing of the sort – at this stage of the proceedings. It's possible there may have been no robbery in the case at all. We must keep our minds open to every possible alternative. It's – it's a delicate matter to hint at; but before we go any further – do you think, perhaps, Sir Justin may have carried the rubies away by mistake, entangled in his clothes? – say, for example, his coat-sleeve?

R: He had never the opportunity! And I know quite well they were there on my neck when he left me, for the last thing he said to me was, looking up at this very window 'That balcony's awfully convenient for a burglary. Mind you take good care of the Remanet rubies.' And I remembered what he'd said when I took them off last night; and that's what makes me so sure I really had them.

G: And you slept with the window open! Well, here we have all the materials, to be sure, for a first-class mystery!

Unit 18   *The Great Ruby Robbery* (2)

18B   *The story continues*

Scene 5: Hyde Park

N: £500 reward offered for recovery of Remanet rubies.

R: Sir Justin!

O: Miss Remanet. Then you don't go to Paris for a while yet – until you get them back?

R: No, Sir Justin; not yet; and – I'm almost glad of it.

O: No, you don't mean that! Well, I confess, Miss Remanet, the first thing I thought myself when I read it in *The Times* was just the very same: Then after all, she won't go yet to Paris.

R: Shall we ride together, Sir Justin?

Scene 6: At Lady Maclure's house

R: It's been ten days now, and this policeman, Gregory, is still in and out of Sir Everard's house as if he owned it. He never misses an opportunity to tell me that the last person on earth one would be likely to suspect is always the one who turns out to have done it. No-one is free from his suspicious eye: Sir Everard, my dear Lady Maclure, the butler, Sir Justin … He will before long, I am sure, accuse myself, or the parrot. I have a feeling that he would dearly like to prove that Sir Justin is the thief, but he's quite wrong there. I know where my own suspicions lie …

Scene 7: Miss Remanet's room

R: Come in.

B: Did you want anything, Miss?

R: Yes. I want to know what you were doing down there outside the front door, prying into other people's letters with the postman. You were there a good ten minutes.

B: The postman's my young man, miss. And we hope before very long now to get married … Will that be all, miss?

R: That'll be all, for now, Bertha.

Scene 8: In the house

M: … I *believe* she's engaged to the postman. I think I heard her say so; though I make it a rule, you see, my dear, to know as little as I can of these people's love affairs. They're so very uninteresting. But Bertha certainly told me she

wouldn't leave me to get married for an indefinite period. That was only ten days ago. She said her young man wasn't just yet in a position to make a home for her.

R: Perhaps something has occurred meanwhile to better her position. Such strange things crop up. She may have come into a fortune!

M: Perhaps so. Though, if so, it must really have been very sudden; for I think it was the morning before you lost your jewels she told me so.

Scene 9: Lady Maclure's dressing room

M: … just a little further to the right, Bertha, please. That's – Ah! Persis!

R: How do these pearls go with my complexion, Lady Maclure?

M: Oh, charming! Never saw anything suit you better, Persis.

R: Except my poor rubies! I wish I could get them back! I wonder that man Gregory hasn't succeeded in finding them.

M: Oh, my dear, you may be sure by this time they're safe in Amsterdam. That's the only place in Europe now to look for them.

B: Why to Amsterdam, my lady?

M: What do you want to know that for, child? Why, to be cut, of course. All the diamond-cutters in the world are concentrated in Amsterdam; and the first thing a thief does when he steals big jewels is to send them across, and have them cut in new shapes so that they can't be identified.

B: I shouldn't have thought they'd have known who to send them to.

M: Why, these things are always done by experienced thieves, who know the ropes well, and are in league with receivers the whole world over. But Gregory has his eye on Amsterdam, I'm sure, and we'll soon hear something.

B: Yes, my lady.

Scene 10: Outside the Maclure house

B: Well? Any news?

P: Yes! A letter from Amsterdam! And I think we've fixed it!

B: Oh Harry! This is too good to be true! Then in just one month we can really get married!

P: It's an awful lot of money! A regular fortune! And what's more, Bertha, if it hadn't been for your cleverness we never should have got it!

B: Well, if I hadn't been so much in love with you, I don't think I could ever have had the wit to manage it. But oh! Harry, when you're in love, you can do *anything*!

Scene 11: The Maclure house

C: Er … Miss Remanet?

R: Yes. You have some news?

C: Your jewels are found, Miss. Will you step round and identify them.

R: Yes, constable. I certainly will.

18C The solution

Scene 12: Police station: Part 1

C: In here, if you please, Miss Remanet, Lady Maclure.

R: Sir Justin. Bertha. Mr Gregory. And …

I: Inspector Johnson, Miss … Miss Remanet – these are your jewels, I believe?

R: Yes. Yes, they are.

I: This is a painful case. A very painful case. We have, I am ashamed to say, conclusive evidence against one of our own men; but as he admits everything, and intends to throw himself on the mercy of the Court, it's no use talking about it. He won't attempt to defend it; indeed, with such evidence, I think he's doing what's best and wisest.

R: I – I don't understand. Who on earth are you talking about? …

Scene 12: Police station: Part 2

I: … and so when Gregory spied your rubies under the corner of the handkerchief, he quietly pocketed them before your very eyes. He felt sure, you see, that nobody could accuse him of a robbery which was committed before he came, and which he had himself been called in to investigate. The worst of it is, he had woven a very ingenious case against Sir Justin O'Byrne, whom we were on the very point of arresting today, if this young woman hadn't come in at the eleventh hour, in the very nick of time, and earned the reward by giving us the clue that led to the discovery and recovery of the jewels. They were brought over this morning by an Amsterdam detective.

R: Bertha!?

B: My young man was the postman, miss. And after what my lady said, I put him up to watch Mr Gregory's delivery for a letter from Amsterdam. I'd suspected him from the very first; and when the letter came, we had him arrested at once, and found out from it who were the people at Amsterdam who had the rubies.

G: Well, I was right, after all, Miss Remanet. I told you the very last person you'd dream of suspecting was sure to be the one that actually did it.

18D Happy ending

Lady O'Byrne's rubies were very much admired at Monte Carlo last season. Mr Gregory has found permanent employment for the next seven years at Her Majesty's prison on the Isle of Portland. Bertha and her postman have retired to Canada with £500 to buy a farm. And everybody says Sir Justin O'Byrne has beaten the record, after all, even for penniless baronets, by making a marriage at once of money and affection.

Unit 19 Family life (2)

19A House rules

EXERCISE 2

1A: There are many points of conflict with Louisa, I think one of the main ones might be an untidy room and untidiness in general. Louisa's generally late for school most mornings even though she leaves the house a good half an hour to 45 minutes later than her sister. So she will tidy her room when she feels like it. It hasn't become a habit, nor can I ever see it becoming a habit, and I was hoping she would use that 45 minutes either – and this is another conflict – to practise her piano or violin or tidy her room. She seems to, now that she's a real teenager at the age of 14, she seems to spend an awful lot of time in bed in the morning, and now she's started putting on make-up.

B: Well, I'm quite lazy, I think, but I mean it's my room and I think that if I want to keep it untidy, cos it's sort of my area, then it's me that's got to live in it, not my parents, but I understand why they want me to keep it tidy, they want me to sort of get into good habits. But I know that, and if I wanted to keep it tidy I would keep it tidy. And getting up in the morning I'm just not a sort of morning person and I think mum is and she's really annoying because she's sort of shout down from upstairs, that actually wakes me up, and that's very annoying.

2B: She doesn't let me watch that much TV after school, which is really annoying because most of my friends watch *Home and Away* and *Neighbours* but I only get to watch one of them. I sometimes don't – I mean I think that's really unfair so sometimes I just watch both anyway.

A: First and foremost, Louisa watches a fair amount of television whether she thinks she's deprived or not, she must watch at least 45 minutes per day. And when I'm not around you know I know the child sneaks in a fair amount more than that. So she she gets in a fair amount of television, certainly on the weekends. But I am of the opinion that television, very very very few programmes will teach them anything. And I think when a child is under your care for 18 years it's the parents' responsibility to make sure that the input is of value, and I don't think television, much television is of any value at all, I think reading a book and doing her piano lessons are far more valuable than watching crummy American soap operas.

3A I just think that living in a huge city like London a child is going to be sophisticated enough by the mere fact that it lives in a city, and that there's plenty of time for growing up and nightclubs and staying out late. Not to mention the fact that I'm fearful of what could happen to them on the streets because as streetwise as they think they are I don't think they're as smart as they think they are and they might get mugged.

B: London, it's, I mean, I'm quite old, well, I'm not but, I'll go out with a group of friends and we'll have about ten of us and you don't really, I mean they sort of say there's safety in numbers and I know it's really dangerous and everything but there's much less chance of me getting mugged if I'm with ten friends than if I'm on my own with my mum.

4A: So I want my child in at a reasonable hour which is flexible for Louisa probably now at the age of 14 between er 10 and 11.30 even. But also there's the fact of homework even though it's a weekend, they've still got homework to do and things to do and I don't want the child to be so tired that she's not going to be able to perform well the next day.

B: I don't get tired that easily, I don't need that much sleep, so but and I can perform well, even if I don't have much sleep. I find I'm more tired when I have more sleep than if I don't have much at all. And I perform well, I think I perform fairly well anyway at school and I'll do my homework, and if I get my homework done then I don't see why there should be a reason that mum wouldn't let me go out – not late, but just to someone else's house or something. Cos just all my other friends are allowed to go to each other's houses and mum won't let me go out on Sundays or weekdays so all I've got really is – and I can't go out on a Friday night because I've got orchestra so all I've got is Saturday. One day of the week when I can go out.

19B *State school or private school?*

EXERCISE 2

B: Like, her views are like really snobby, sometimes, and she calls me a reverse snob sometimes, but I don't think I am. Cos she prefers the private school system to the state school system, which is fair enough because she wants the best for me but I'd sort of rather stay where I am because I'm moving schools, you see, to a private school from a state school.

A: I think there's, you know, some truth in that. I think the child is probably right about my snobbery. Um I'm very very confused about the education in this country and I don't like the system at all. I went to a comprehensive myself, my husband went to a grammar school, and I feel that mixed education is ultimately the best but in England you come out with a new statistic every week saying single sex education show better results, and ultimately I thought if we've got the

money to pay for the best for our child we've got to decide what we think is the best. And we had long long talks about it, and ultimately decided that private school was best. But yes, there's a bit of snobbery in there as well in that I think living in a big city parents with money tend to send their kids to private school and I found myself often the only one sending my children to comprehensive and I found it hard to keep on explaining although most of the best people I know, many of my friends do send their children to local school and I like them probably better than I like some of the parents who send their children to private schools. It's a big mess.

She loves her school, she's very very popular, she's doing very well academically and um she doesn't want to go quite rightly. So my husband and I understood entirely her anger and we just had to keep our heads down and deal with it. We sent her for reasons that we're not even quite sure of ourselves. So it's very difficult trying to explain it to a 14-year-old. But we thought the music was better at this private school, we thought that she could stay at this private school till she was 18 and the private school has done well by our 17-year-old, so even though it's more dull and doesn't have boys we thought she might do better all round at this private school.

B: I think being in a comprehensive school with boys and girls I mean it might, if you want to do well at a comprehensive then you will do well, and you'll always get, you're going to get sort of mixed people but you get a much wider range of nationalities and cultures and stuff in a comprehensive school than you will in a private school. Because if you went to a private school you get basically the same type of person you know they're all sort of middle class, they've got a fair amount of money and they're all quite intelligent. Whereas if you go to a comprehensive school, like I do, then you'll see sort of all types of people, and it just adapts you more to the real world, that you'll be much more likely to be able to cope with all different types of people when you're out of school. And boys, boys do not distract me at all, I mean I'm friends with most of them, well all of them so I mean they don't distract me and um they're just like girls to me but they're boys. I think Mum's just got this thing and I think she does want to look quite good in front of other people. I think that's one of the main reasons, when I have to say where I go to school to some people. Mum didn't like it because all their kids go to private schools and she just wants the best for me anyway and she thinks that maybe – cos, I'm good at working but I need to be pushed, and private schools push you much more than comprehensives. So she thinks that perhaps Notting Hill would be much better for me which is a private school. Because it would push me and it would just, Mum says if we've got the money we might as well use it to give you the best education. She wants what's best for me later on. So, I can't really complain.

Unit 20   *Here*

20A   *The poem*

EXERCISE 2

See page 65.

20B   *An interpretation*

EXERCISE 1

This is a poem by Philip Larkin called *Here*, and it describes Philip Larkin's journey by train travelling north up through England, and his impressions on leaving the Midlands and the South and arriving almost at the east coast, near Hull, which is where my parents live, and where I've lived for nearly 20 years. And he describes the depressing grey industrial towns as he's travelling through on the train. And then he describes the River Humber, as he's moving round towards the east on the train, and he describes the birds, the gulls in the mud75
. And then he describes the city itself and the barges, and it's an old dock city. And then he describes the people, the women in their cheap, he uses the word *cheap*, cheap clothing, and he talks about these department stores with these glass swinging doors. His tone is slightly sarcastic and I think snobbish in a way. He's gone up to greater things and he's going back home. And in a way I can relate to this. It seems so provincial going back up to the east of England now, he talks about the suburban areas outside the city and then the isolated villages beyond this suburban sprawl, and that's where I spent a large part of my childhood in a village almost in the middle of nowhere. And he mentions the loneliness of these villages, sort of surrounded by wheatfields which are shadowed by the darkness of the city. And I agree with him entirely, his impressions bring it all back, makes me homesick.

EXERCISE 3

The reason this poem appeals to me is that I can completely visualise Larkin's journey as he moves north, and I've had the same feelings of going back in time, going back to my roots and childhood. I've had similar impressions of how the countryside becomes so much more provincial, more conservative, in people's clothing, people's behaviour. People becoming very open and I think very friendly. It's something I really do associate with this part of the world. Yeah, I do feel incredibly nostalgic about the north of England. I miss it greatly, miss the warmth of the people, the homeliness of living in this village in the middle of a field. But at the same time, going back there, as Larkin describes, seems to be a digression, going back to something I've left behind me, as if I've stepped away from the narrow-mindedness maybe of the small tightly-knit community. And I'm glad to have got out of it, but do miss all these things.

To the teacher

This book is the fourth in the *Cambridge Skills for Fluency* series. It continues the approach to listening featured in the first three levels of the series, and has three main aims:
- to provide *opportunities* to listen to a wide variety of natural spoken English, presented in a way that is motivating and accessible to advanced learners;
- to develop learners' listening *skills* by helping them to draw on their own natural strategies for listening effectively;
- to provide an *active* approach to listening which integrates listening with other skills.

In order to build on the skills developed in the earlier books in the series, *Listening 4* presents additional challenges to learners, who are assumed to be at upper-intermediate to advanced level. Features of the book include:
- longer and often faster stretches of spoken English, and some recordings where the speaker is heard over natural background noise;
- more activities in which students are asked to focus precisely on factual details, vocabulary or style;
- a wider variety of different speakers and accents;
- more opportunities for discussion, both before and after listening to the recordings;
- a wider range of topics and types of listening, including topics of general interest, discussion issues, excerpts from radio broadcasts, poetry, drama, songs and technical descriptions.

Listening strategies

A fundamental idea underlying this book is that listening is not merely a 'passive' or 'receptive' skill; rather that when we listen, we naturally employ a variety of active 'strategies' (e.g. predicting, matching against our own experience, distinguishing important from unimportant information, inferring information about the speaker), which help us to make sense of what we are listening to.

These strategies are referred to in the Map of the book on pages 4–5. We have not regarded them as discrete 'skills' that can or need to be taught; we see them rather as an underlying resource that students already have in their own language, and which they can draw on to help them listen to English.

The recordings

Most of the recordings are of unscripted, spontaneous English, spoken by 'real' people (not simulated by actors). The recordings of radio items, stories, drama, poetry and song (in Units 1, 4, 8, 9, 14, 17, 18 and 20) are either taken from original sources or are recreated by actors in a studio. The recordings feature a variety of voices and speaking styles, including:
- children and teenagers as well as adults;
- a range of British regional accents, including Scottish, Northern English, London and South-West English;
- American, Australian, and Indian varieties of English;
- non-native speakers of English (French, Dutch, German and Serbo-Croat speakers).

Using the book

Structure of the book

The book contains 20 units. Each unit provides material for an hour or more of class listening and associated activities. Units begin with two or three main sections (A, B and sometimes C). In some units these sections belong closely together and develop a single theme through the unit; in others they can be used more or less independently, and deal with different aspects of a topic. The final section in each unit (C or D) provides extension activities in which students can use what they have listened to as a basis for creative speaking or writing.

Listening in class

This book is mainly designed to be used in class, and this is reflected in the active approach we have taken to listening. Although the main focus of each unit is on listening, this is integrated into a range of oral (and sometimes written) activities. Each section begins with a pre-listening activity, to introduce the topic and prepare students for the listening, and most of the listening tasks themselves are open-ended to encourage students to discuss, comment, interpret and react, as well as merely to record information.

Self-study listening

Although the book is mainly intended for use in class, many of the activities can be done by students working alone with the cassette, either at home or in a self-access room or language laboratory, using the transcript at the end of the book as an answer key. As each unit is divided into sections, it would also be possible to cover some sections of each unit in class, and leave others for students to work through on their own outside class time.

We hope this book will help your students to listen to English effectively, and that both you and they enjoy using the material.

Acknowledgements

We are very grateful to the following people who have helped in developing this book:

Lindsay White for her patience, understanding and encouragement throughout the writing of the book.

Our editor, Elizabeth Sharman, for her work on the final typescript, and Amanda Ogden for her help with the pilot material.

Studio AVP, London, for their assistance with the recordings, and for producing the final cassette.

Tibor Lévay for his technical help and advice.

Christine Gowdridge of the British Council, Munich, Ian Russell of Box Church of England Primary School, and Carolyn Becket for their help in arranging recordings.

We would like to thank the following people who contributed to the recordings:

Sarah Cox	David Hill	Paula Preskett
Bryan Cruden	Hazel Jones	Paul Roberts
Eve Cruden	Anastasia Katsikiotis	Philippe Roy
Roger Da Silva	Judith Martin	Adrienne Smith
Helen Derbyshire	Davinda Matharou	Jessica Stubbings
John Flory	Nan Mulder	William Tribe
George and Jan Gynn	Dobrila Nastić	Zdenka Tribe
Harold Hayes	Graham Preskett	Gabriela Zaharias
Adrian Head	Louisa Preskett	

... and the children of the Box Church of England Primary School, Wiltshire, and of Towerbank Primary School, Edinburgh, who told the jokes in Unit 14.

We would also like to thank the teachers at the following institutions, where *Listening 4* was piloted, for all their constructive suggestions without which the improvements in the book would not have been made:

ELF, Edinburgh; CIC School of English, Barcelona; Eurocentre, Cambridge; ELCRA-Bell S·A·, Geneva; Lake School of English, Oxford; British Institute, Florence; Dominic Fisher.

The authors and publishers are grateful to the following for permission to reproduce copyright material:

Lyrics of *Low Self Opinion* by the Henry Rollins Band in Unit 9 are reproduced by permission of BMG Music Publishing Limited. Words and music by Chris Haskett, Simon Cain McDonald, Henry Rollins and Andrew Weiss. Copyright © Imago Music Inc; The transcript of *The Bricklayer* from *Gerard Hoffnung – Speech at the Oxford Union December 1958* in Unit 14 is reproduced courtesy of the British Broadcasting Corporation; *Here* from *Collected Poems* by Philip Larkin in Unit 20 is reprinted by permission of Faber and Faber Ltd and Farrar, Straus and Giroux Inc. Copyright © 1988, 1989 by the Estate of Philip Larkin.

Recordings: St Ivel advertisement in Unit 3 is courtesy of Air Edel; GWR excerpts in Unit 8 courtesy of Dirk Anthony at GWR FM, Bristol, Wiltshire and Bath; Recorded extract of *Low Self Opinion* by the Henry Rollins Band in Unit 9 is reproduced by permission of BMG Records (UK) Limited; Recorded extract of *The Bricklayer* from *Gerard Hoffnung – Speech at the Oxford Union December 1958* in Unit 14 is reproduced courtesy of the British Broadcasting Corporation.

Photographs: The Kobal Collection (p6 left, p16); Aquarius Literary Agency and Picture Library (p6 top right, p6 bottom right, p31 top right); Twentieth Century Fox (p7); Christopher Jones (p12); J Allan Cash (p13 A, p18 left, p27, p46); The Telegraph Colour Library (p13 B); Nigel Luckhurst (p13 C, D, E, p68); Impact Photos (p17, p35); Camera Press (p20 top, p36 left, p36 right); The Architectural Association (p20 bottom); Western Daily Press (p29); Famous (p31 left, p31 bottom right); BMG Records (UK) Limited (p32, p33); The Press Association Photo Library (p34 top); Hulton Deutsch (p34 bottom, p67 C, p67 G); Barnaby's Picture Library (p37, pp40 + 41 publicans, p66 B); Valerie Cooper (p40 main picture); Jeremy Pembrey (pp40 + 41 vicar); Image Bank (pp40 + 41 butcher, pp40 + 41 schoolgirl, pp40 + 41 chef, pp40 + 41 teacher, p67 E); Tony Stone Images (p44, p63 left, p63 right, p67 D, p67 F); Université de Liège (p52 top); Patrick Pye (p52 bottom); Herman Gordijn (p53 top); Nan Mulder (p54); Sean Hudson (p56); Kingston upon Hull City Council (p66 A).

The publishers are unable to trace the copyright holders of the following material, and would be grateful for any information that would enable them to do so:

Dracula recording in Unit 1 originally published by Zeus Publishing; *The Island* in Unit 4 originally recorded on Caedmon Audiocassettes.

Drawings by Rowan Barnes Murphy (p8), Phil Healey (pp11, p46, p47, p49, p62); Karou Myake (pp15, p16); Trevor Ridley (pp22, p23); Eric Rowe (p24); Peter Byatt (p25, p37, p50) Trevor Parkin (p38); Leslie Marshall (p39, p48); Tony Morris (p57, p58, p60, p61). Other artwork by Peter Ducker.

Book design by Peter Ducker MSTD